SECTION 106 AND GAME THEORY

SECTION 106 AND GAME THEORY

Joseph Y. Garrison

To my clients. You showed me the true meaning of heritage stewardship.

Copyright © 2016 by Joseph Y. Garrison
All rights reserved.
ISBN-13: 978-1537622903
ISBN-10: 1537622900

CONTENTS

INTRODUCTION — 13

THE SECTION 106 REVIEW RULE BOOK — 16

PART ONE:
GAME THEORY IN CONTEXT — 18

THE SOURCES OF MY RESEARCH — 18
DEFINITIONS, DOCTRINE, AND PLAYERS — 21
DESCARTES AND THE IMPERATIVE OF PROOF — 25

PART TWO:
MODERN GAME THEORY — 29

MODERN GAME THEORY AND CONFLICT RESOLUTION — 29
'ANALOGOUS PREDICTIVE ANALYSIS' AND BRINKMANSHIP — 31

'ANALOGOUS PREDICTIVE ANALYSIS' IN MORE DETAIL	36
IF-THEN STATEMENTS	38
DOMINATED AND DOMINANT STRATEGIES	40
WORDS	41
GOALS AND STRATEGIES / UTILITY THEORY	43
JAKE NIELSON AND DOMINANT GOALS	49
GOALS AND STRATEGIES / PROSPECT THEORY	55
RATIONAL/HONORABLE AND IRRATIONAL/DISHONORABLE GAME STRATEGIES	61
MAXIMS	64
INDUCEMENTS AND RESTRICTIONS	67
THE INFLUENCE OF 'COMMON KNOWLEDGE'	70
'FOCAL POINTS'	72
INFLUENCES THAT PRE-DETERMINE THE COURSE OF THE GAME	74
GRAPHICAL TOOLS	77
A CHALLENGE TO GAME THEORY: PROFESSOR STANLEY K. RIDGLEY	83

ACKNOWLEDGED LIMITS — 85

INTERLUDE:
THE PRISONER'S DILEMMA — 87

PART THREE:
GAME THEORY AND SECTION 106 REVIEW — 90

TRUSTING GAME THEORY'S USEFULNESS IN SECTION 106 REVIEW — 90
IS IT REALLY A GAME? — 92
'ANALOGOUS PREDICTIVE ANALYSIS' MODELING — 95
CATEGORIES BY OBJECT OF THE GAME — 96
A GAME OF SEQUENCE — 99
CATALOGUED BY TYPE — 100
RULES, PLAYERS, SUCCESSIVE ROUNDS, BIDDING SEQUENCE, AND ANALYSIS OF PLAY — 107
THE NASH EQUILIBRIUM — 121

PART FOUR: THE GREAT LESSONS   126

'SYMMETRY AND PARITY'   126
SECTION 106 REVIEW AND 'SYMMETRY AND PARITY'   126
SPECIFIC LESSONS LEARNED FROM PROFESSOR ARTHUR T. BERNJAMIN   137
A VINDICATION OF GAME THEORY: ROBERT AXELROD   143
 USING THE 'TIT FOR TAT' STRATEGY   148
'TIT FOR TAT' AND THE 'GRIM TRIGGER'   151
'THE EVOLUTION OF COOPERATION'   153
THE MOST IMPORTANT LESSON   160
OVER THE LONG HAUL   161
CHAOS THEORY   163

INTERLUDE: PROMOTING COOPERATION DEFENDS THE PROCESS   **166**

THE ULTIMATE RESOLUTION OF CONFLICT WITHIN THE 36 CFR 800 RULES: DRASTIC MEASURES   **168**

CODA   **170**

THE TAKEAWAY   **176**

POSTSCRIPT   **179**

APPENDIX 'A': A Case Study: A Section 106 Review Game Played According To The Rules Codified At 36 CFR 800.3-.6   181

APPENDIX 'B': Game Theory And Section 106 Quick Reference   206

INTRODUCTION

"The game is more than the player of the game."
- Rudyard Kipling

"I can explain this to you; I can't comprehend it for you."
- Edward Koch

I am now retired, but for more than thirty years, I worked in the field of environmental review and compliance as Review and Compliance Coordinator for the Tennessee State Historic Preservation Office. During that time, I witnessed more than my share of instances where cooperation among the participants in a specific case review would have been much more beneficial in attaining their mutual goals than the competition, confrontation, and conflict that actually occurred. In one unfortunate case, the continuing inability of the participants to put aside their competitive and conflicting goals in favor of more cooperative ones prolonged the successful resolution of a case by twenty years.

I am convinced the tenets of Heritage Stewardship contained within the National Historic Preservation Act (NHPA) and written into its Section 106 review process gain nothing from such conflicted cases.

With that conviction in mind, I began what became a wide-ranging investigation of an assortment of trustworthy approaches to resolving conflict. Among the more traditional methods I have studied are negotiation, mediation, arbitration, and litigation. Admittedly, these methods of dispute resolution all have valuable lessons to teach. However, none offered me much in the way of practical guidance that would help me *prevent* conflict in my own Heritage Stewardship work. Finally, however, I believe I have found such a method; Game Theory.

SECTION 106 AND GAME THEORY

This book considers how State Historic Preservation Office Environmental Review and Compliance (R&C) staffers, and Federal Agency Officials, and applicants for Federal assistance can best use the analysis of the Section 106 review process made possible by modern Game Theory's mathematical modeling to assist them in resolving and preventing those conflicts that occasionally erupt out of their cases. Furthermore, I believe all those additional Consulting Parties named in the Section 106 review rulebook (36 CFR 800) will also benefit from the information contained in this book.

No one associated with the Section 106 review process needs either the mindset or the training of a Game Theory mathematician to comprehend that discipline's basic tenets concerning highest goals and the strategies for attaining them. There are today countless practitioners schooled in a great variety of disciplines who are attempting to resolve conflict of one sort or another by using Game Theory's strategies to attain their goals. My study of the various strategies they have used has brought me to the conclusion that modern Game Theory provides the most likely of all for attaining success.

This book is my bid to pass along what I have learned about the usefulness of modern Game Theory so that readers may use its lessons to resolve and even prevent conflict in Section 106 review cases. In making this bid, I must presume that they wish as deeply as I do to avoid those conflicts that militate against the successful completion of Section 106 reviews. If that is the case, I hope they find this book useful. I have also, from time to time, inserted some tangential material in the form of "Author's Notes" that I hope will entertain as well as educate.

Section 106 Review Basics / A Recap

For those who need a quick refresher, Section 106 of the National Historic Preservation Act (NHPA) obliges Federal agencies to take National Register of Historic Places (NRHP) listed or eligible Historic Properties into account as they plan and carry out any project, program, or activity that might cause an effect to those Historic Properties. Section 106 refers to such activities as 'Undertakings'. Undertakings are those "projects, programs, or activities funded in whole or in part under the direct or indirect jurisdiction of a Federal agency, including those carried out by or on behalf of a Federal agency; those carried out with Federal financial assistance; and those requiring a Federal permit, license, or approval".

When taking Historic Properties into account relative to a particular Undertaking, an agency-selected Federal Agency Official must first consult with the appropriate State Historic Preservation Officer/Tribal Historic Preservation Officer (SHPO/THPO) and other Consulting Parties to identify and evaluate all 'Cultural Resources' located within a Federal project's Area of Potential Effects (APE). The National Park Service defines a Cultural Resource as "a building, structure, district, site, object, or definite location of human activity, occupation, or use recognizable through field survey, historical documentation, or oral evidence. Cultural Resources are prehistoric, historic, archaeological, or architectural sites, structures, places, or objects and traditional religious or cultural properties". Evaluated Historic Properties *are* Cultural Resources determined eligible for listing in the NRHP.

If the Cultural Resources assessment made by the Agency Official determines that Cultural Resources are located within the Undertaking's APE, **then** the Federal Agency Official must consult with the appropriate

SHPO/THPO to evaluate their National Register of Historic Places (NRHP / National Register)) eligibility using the Criteria of Eligibility codified at 36 CFR 63. **If** both agree that a Cultural Resource *is* National Register eligible, **then** the Agency Official must consult with the SHPO/THPO to assess any potential for her Undertaking to affect that NRHP eligible or listed Historic Property adversely using the 'Criteria of Adverse Effect' codified at 36 CFR 800.5. **If** this assessment results in a finding that an adverse effect will occur, **then** the Federal Agency Official must consult with the SHPO/THPO and others about the best ways to resolve that adverse effect.

This four-step process encompasses everything that is essential to compliant Section 106 review.

THE SECTION 106 REVIEW RULE BOOK

"You have to learn the rules of the game. And then you have to play better than anyone else."
- Albert Einstein

All processes have rules that govern how those processes should proceed properly, and Section 106 review is no exception. The most important ruleset for that process comes from Section 106 of the NHPA itself. Here it is in paraphrase once again:

Section 106 *requires* Federal agencies to take into account the effects of their Undertakings on Historic Properties, and afford the Advisory Council on Historic Preservation a reasonable opportunity to comment.

Because of Section 106, those Federal agencies that plan projects, programs, or activities that might cause an effect to a Historic Property will be playing the game of Section 106 review whether they want to or not. Once an agency representative has come to the Section 106 consultation table, she, along with all other participants, is required to play by the specific ruleset published in the Federal Register by the Advisory Council on Historic Preservation (ACHP). This ruleset is referred to by its title, "Protection of Historic Properties" / 36 CFR 800. The current version became effective on August 5, 2004.

This Section 106 review ruleset contains the official order of regulations governing the process, specifying how each Federal agency carries out its statutory requirements under NHPA.

The Federal Regulation / 36 CFR 800:

1) requires each Federal agency to name **a Federal Agency Official** responsible for carrying out each of its Undertakings by a formal submission of certain determinations and findings ('bids') to the other players for their review and comment
2) lists the **various participants** to whom the Agency Official must 'bid' those project-related determinations and findings for review and comment. These participants have an acknowledged and legitimate stake in the review process (legal standing). They are the SHPO/THPO and other named Consulting Parties
3) describes a set of **four successive rounds** ('Steps') of review play during which the Agency Official submits those determinations and findings and during which those stakeholders review and comment upon them

4) describes the **support documentation** that the Agency Official must submit to justify her determinations and findings

5) itemizes all **allowable determinations and findings** ('bids') that may be arrived at by the Agency Official, the SHPO/THPO, and, at times, other participants.

6) offers an **allowable range of strategies** that all participants in the process may use to attain an allowable range of goals during review, and

7) stipulates an **allowable set of outcomes** ('payoffs') that will document compliant completion of the process

I must assume any reader interested enough in the Section 106 review process to read this book is familiar with that process to the point of understanding the examples presented in the text.

PART ONE: GAME THEORY IN CONTEXT

THE SOURCES OF MY RESEARCH

"All I'm armed with is research."
- *Mike Wallace*

A great deal of what I have learned about Game Theory I gained from reading *Game Theory, A Nontechnical Introduction* by Morton D. Davis (Dover Publications, Inc., 1983). Davis (Professor Emeritus of Mathematics at the City College of New York) writes that Game Theorists study the ways rational participants ('players') make decisions while playing a simple, two-person board game such as Checkers and then use mathematical modeling to propose ways these and other players might make *better* decisions while playing that same game in the future. Furthermore, modern Game Theory proposes that this better decision making can also improve results in more "high stakes" games that have proven to be analogous to the simple two-person board games for which they already have derivations.

Morton Davis argues that anyone who has ever played a game knows that some moves ('dominant' moves) *always* prove to be better than others ('dominated' moves) do and modern Game Theory modeling uses mathematics in an attempt to reveal which are which. Once this modeling has separated winning strategies from losing ones in simple, two-person games, Game Theory proposes that these same strategies may be applied successfully in the more "high stakes" analogous games they have identified.

Next. To my mind, one of the best current explanations of the various kinds of games Game Theorists use as test benches to assess the soundness of their models is *Game Theory 101: The Complete Textbook* by William Spaniel (2011-2015, William Spaniel). Mr. Spaniel (PhD candidate in political science at the University of Rochester) thoroughly analyses such key benchmark games as "The Prisoner's Dilemma" and "Rock, Paper, Scissors", clearly illustrating his analyses with game trees and payoff matrixes (more about these later). Furthermore, he explains both the basic and the complex ideas of Game Theory in language readily understood by laymen such as I am.

Next. Presh Talwalkar (who runs the YouTube channel and blog "Mind Your Decisions"), delivers a handy general introduction to the topic in *The Joy Of Game Theory: An Introduction to Strategic Thinking*, (ND, self-published). Like Spaniel, Talwalkar's writing style de-mystifies much of the method of Game Theory and offers clear examples of its various principles. The aim of his book is to help readers recognize strategic situations in their daily lives and to use Game Theory modeling to make those decisions better.

Next. Dr. Stanley K. Ridgley (Assistant Professor, Department of Management at Drexel University's LeBow College of Business) offers an insightful discussion of Game Theory in a series of video lectures entitled "Strategic Thinking Skills" (The Great Courses, 2012). Dr. Ridgley states, "When people interact with each other, they are playing games". He defines games as "interdependent interactions among rational people moved to make the best of a set of allowable moves ('strategies') by their desire to attain certain goals ('payoffs', 'utilities')". According to Ridgley, the art/science of Game Theory offers practical assistance when these "rational people [must] reason when presented with dilemmas that provide incomplete information".

Next. Dr. Scott P. Stevens (Professor of Computer Information Systems and Management Science at James Madison University) gives us a rather comprehensive treatment of Game Theory in a series of video lectures entitled "Games People Play: Game Theory in Life, Business, and Beyond" (The Great Courses, 2008). Stevens' main emphasis is upon the uses of Game Theory in Economics. However, many of his assertions about the discipline remain useful to us within the specific context of Section 106 review.

Next. Yet another valuable resource is a series of video lectures by Dr. Arthur T. Benjamin, "The Mathematics of Games and Puzzles: From Cards to Sudoku," (The Great Courses, 2013). Dr. Benjamin (Professor of Mathematics at Harvey Mudd College) teaches many of the more complicated principles of Game Theory graphically in a way this layman can easily understand.

Next. My final and most illuminating source of insight into the realm of Game Theory is the authoritative and influential book, *The Evolution of Cooperation*, by Robert Axelrod (Basic Books, 1984). Axelrod (Professor of Political Science and Public Policy at the University of Michigan) used a computer tournament participated in by a number of our planet's foremost Game Theorists to discover the best strategy that promises ultimate cooperation among game participants. Then he shared that winning strategy in his book.

Beyond researching these seven key sources on Game Theory, I have read widely in the discipline of conflict resolution and have combined what I have recently learned about Game Theory's role in that area with my more than thirty years of direct experience in Section 106 review. In doing so, I have prepared a roadmap that will lead a discerning reader toward the successful completion of even the most controversial Section 106 review cases.

DEFINITIONS, DOCTRINE, AND PLAYERS

"The game has a cleanness. If you do a good job, the numbers say so."
- Sandy Koufax

Game Theory General Definitions

The *Oxford Dictionaries* website defines Game Theory as, "that branch of mathematics concerned with the analysis of strategies for dealing with competitive situations where the outcome of a participant's choice of action depends critically upon the actions of other participants". To determine players' best winning outcomes in certain games, Game Theory uses models to gauge those interdependent strategies mathematically. Morton Davis refines that definition. He defines Game Theory as the art/science of "mathematical modeling that accurately forecasts the outcomes of specific interactions among intelligent, rational decision-makers where there is a clear choice between conflict and cooperation". Scott Stevens' definition is even more straightforward and broad-based. For him, Game Theory is "the study of strategic, interactive decision making among rational decision makers". Ariel D. Procaccia (Assistant Professor, Computer Science Department, Carnegie Mellon University) may have found the simplest and most direct definition of all. She writes, "We interpret a 'game' as a *strategic interaction* between two or more rational players."

Some purists insist that any application of Game Theory modeling, concepts, and techniques should be confined to board and card games. Applying Game Theory analysis to 'non-game' activities such as economics, armed conflict, or government is nothing except 'gamification' of 'high stakes' interactions that have little in common with the board and card games Game Theorists model. According to Wikipedia, the term "gamification" was coined in 2002 by Nick Pelling, a British-born computer programmer and inventor, and has come into more general use since 2010. However, this book will adopt Scott Stevens' broad-based definition of games and Game Theory. The majority of mathematicians who propose the sort of modeling that *quantifies* Game Theory's interactive decisions refer to all such interactions as 'games,' and, therefore, so shall I.

Admittedly, games for which predictive mathematical models currently exist lean toward one-person (Solitaire), or two-person games (Tic-Tac-Toe, Checkers, NIM, Rock-Paper-Scissors, etc.). Today, approximately 29 such board and card games have complete derivations (admittedly many of these games are quite obscure and un-familiar to the general reader).

Therefore, for those who must prevent or resolve conflict in complex human interactions such as Section 106 review, it might appear that such models *would* have little relevance. However, since the 1970s, Game Theorists have proved conclusively that the same mathematical principles that accurately predict winning play in two-person 'low stakes' games can be used with a fair degree of accuracy to predict winning play in *analogous* 'high-stakes' games as well. I will spend a great deal of the rest of this book discussing the implications of *'analogous'*.

Author's Note – Do not bother to search for Game Theory modeling analyses of games of pure chance such as dice throwing games, Roulette, Chuck-a-Luck and so forth, because rational players' strategies do not interdepend upon those of other players and chance itself overcomes any rationality individual players might bring to the game.

The Game Theory Doctrine: 'Analogous Predictive Analysis'

Various dictionaries define the word "analogous" slightly differently, but, in essence, analogous things are similar to each other in some way and therefore comparable in certain respects. Simply put, they are things that perform a similar function but have a different origin. Predictive analytics deals with extracting information from data and using it to predict trends and behavior patterns. Put together, Game Theory's 'analogous predictive analysis' extracts information from the data set of known 'low stakes' games and uses it to predict trends and behavior patterns in analogous 'high stakes' games whose function is similar and comparable while admittedly having different origins.

SECTION 106 AND GAME THEORY

According to the mathematical models Game Theorists have created over the past forty-odd years, certain kinds of games, whether 'low-stakes' or 'high-stakes', will have enough core elements in common to make them amenable to analogous predictive analysis. Within those classifiable and comparable categories of games, strategies and goals that have been determined best in a low-stakes game such as Checkers being played by "cutthroat" old friends may be equally derived in high-stakes games such as Operational Theater Level Warfare being played by two opposing superpowers. Comparable games may range all the way from simple, two-person games such as Tic-Tac-Toe up to theater-level conflicts participated in by two conventional military alliances. Think of it this way, according to analogous predictive analysis, "eggs is eggs, regardless of size".

Game Theory: Rational Players

For their modeling to operate successfully, Game Theory's disciples expect *rational* players to play any game that is susceptible of analogous predictive analysis. Accordingly, one must then ask, "what exactly is meant by the term, 'rational'"? Dr. Scott Stevens defines a 'rational' player as "one who chooses [her] goals and strategies based upon an awareness of [her] best possible *expected* payoff, given [her] knowledge of the game-related situation at the time those choices were made and also the choices of the other players". According to Stevens, rational players will select intelligent goals and strategies before the game begins and modify them at distinct points during game play because of their interaction with other players. As a result, the goals and strategies chosen by a rational player *may*, and at times, *must* change as play moves forward. Anyone who has ever player Checkers knows the validity of this approach.

DESCARTES AND THE IMPERATIVE OF PROOF

"If you would be a real seeker after truth, it is necessary that at least once in your life you doubt, as far as possible, all things."
   - *René Descartes*

"Cogito ergo sum" (French: Je pense, donc je suis; I think, therefore I am).
   - *René Descartes*

Game Theory owes a great deal of its philosophical confirmation as well as its operational method to the work of René Descartes (31 March 1596 – 11 February 1650). Descartes is ranked among the foremost of the French Renaissance's mathematicians and is generally acknowledged as the father of modern philosophy.

Descartes dedicated many years of his life to the solution of certain basic philosophical mysteries. His principal strategy for clearing away the obstacles blocking that pursuit involved higher mathematical modeling. At some point in his life, Descartes became convinced that a verifiable mathematical proof was the only truly trustworthy means of confirming the accuracy of any solution that had been obtained mathematically. Based upon this conviction, Descartes put forward the much bolder and more fundamental philosophical proposal that one could use mathematics as a reliable tool to unlock the secrets hidden within *all* fields of human knowledge so long as a verifiable mathematical proof supported any mathematical solution one claimed to be valid. Still later in life, Descartes went even further by insisting that **if** one *could* use mathematics that way, **then** one *should* do so.

Descartes' firm commitment to mathematical analysis as the most trustworthy means of unlocking the door to truth eventually compelled him to reject the precedent-bound, rigid, and repressive epistemological worldview of the "School Men" (1100-1700). Their belief systems, based almost entirely upon Aristotelian logic and the experiential writings of the early Church Fathers, had reigned supreme at the most influential European universities ever since medieval times. Their influence, both secular and ecclesiastical, had risen to its apogee during Descartes' own lifetime.

Scholasticism's followers held to both a theology and a philosophy that insisted obdurately that tradition and belief were the sole authorities concerning what one may know about truth. To them, the demand for mathematical proof, such as proposed by Descartes, was wholly un-necessary and even bordered on the sacrilegious. Their worldview left little room for a 'Doubting Thomas' such as Descartes, and, not surprisingly, his own worldview left little room for them.

Whatever philosophical differences existed between Descartes and the School Men, he was well aware that he must temper his criticism of them because they had such ways and means of countering criticism that could silence the critic as well as the criticism.

Scholasticism's chief instrument in Western Europe for disciplining the "unruly" was the Roman Inquisition. The Roman Inquisition, formally the Supreme Sacred Congregation of the Roman and Universal Inquisition, was composed of a system of tribunals deployed in various European countries by the Holy See of the Roman Catholic Church. These tribunals held sway during the second half of the 16th. Century and the first half of the 17th. Century. They were charged with the responsibility of prosecuting individuals accused of a wide array of crimes relating to alternate religious doctrine or alternate religious beliefs.

Author's Note - Galileo Galilei (15 February 1564[3] – 8 January 1642), the "Father of Science", was a contemporary of Descartes. His astronomical observations led to his propounding the notion that the earth revolved around the sun, (heliocentric theory) and not vice versa. This theory was 'investigated' by the Roman Inquisition in 1615. That august and powerful body concluded that heliocentrism was "foolish and absurd in philosophy, and formally heretical since it explicitly contradicts in many places the sense of Holy Scripture". Descartes lived throughout his career within this repressive intellectual environment. When, in 1633, the Catholic Church condemned Galileo, Descartes abandoned plans to publish his *Treatise on the World*, his work painstakingly prepared over the previous four years.

In place of Scholasticism, with its devotion to belief, faith, logic, and precedent, Descartes substituted the principle that uncertainty, doubt, and the resulting demand for practical proof must mark the proper starting point along any path a seeker could trust eventually to lead to truth. Descartes' guiding principal was, "never to accept anything for true which I did not clearly know to be such." His device for capturing that necessary proof and his greatest legacy to today's cadre of Games Theorists came to be known as 'Cartesian Analysis' or 'Analytic Geometry'.

During and after Descartes' lifetime, his disciples collected all his extant derivative mathematical formulas and their proofs into a priceless set of algebraic theorems that propose universal properties of equivalence plus an equally worthy companion set of geometric postulates. Modern Game Theorists have built upon these theorems to puzzle out the winning strategies and highest goals of today's games.

Descartes' profound contribution to modern epistemological thought is the revolutionary manner in which he mingled the abstractions of algebra and the concretions of geometry together through the Cartesian coordinate system. Theoretically, modern mathematicians can follow Descartes' example and use algebraic formulas to express already known geometrical values to puzzle out an as-yet-unknown best outcome for *any* two-player interaction.

Game Theory refers to a game's best outcome as **'utility'**. It defines **utility** as, a *mathematically expressible* **highest value or lowest risk**. Through a painstaking use of and expansion upon Cartesian Analysis, Game Theorists have the ability to identify many of these utilities through the analysis of the known geometric relationships found within comparable games.

PART TWO: MODERN GAME THEORY

MODERN GAME THEORY AND CONFLICT RESOLUTION

"If past history was all there was to the game, the richest people would be librarians."
- *Warren Buffett*

"In mathematics you don't understand things. You just get used to them."
- *John von Neumann*

Until the end of the Second World War, the 'war game' constraints placed upon Game Theory up until that time dominated the thinking of its foremost disciples. That all changed dramatically in 1944 with the birth of what scholars in the field have chosen to call 'modern' Game Theory. That year, Oskar Morgenstern and John von Neumann published *Theory of Games and Economic Behavior* (Princeton University Press, 1944). In this book, Morgenstern and von Neumann used Cartesian Analysis to suggest a *mathematically analogous relationship* between how the card game, Poker, is played and how key economic decisions are arrived at. This amazing line of inquiry shifted the focus of Game Theory far away from the development of ever-more-intricate and rigid 'war game' scenarios and more closely toward the Cartesian Analysis of two-player board and card games with the intent of using that analysis to prevent or peacefully resolve the very confrontational situations upon which traditional Game Theory had been focused.

This fresh emphasis has made Game Theory considerably more suitable for analytical use within the social, political, economic, behavioral, and even biological sciences where peaceful conflict resolution is a common goal. The concept of "winning" has shifted away from the 'null-set/I win, you lose' paradigm of the "war games" and toward something much more appealing to those persons tasked with the responsibility of resolving and preventing conflict.

After the publication of von Neumann and Morgenstern's seminal book, psychologists, economists, sociologists, jurists, political scientists, biologists, diplomatists, and specialists in a host of similar worldly disciplines came to seek help from these Game Theorizing mathematicians and their disciples.

Simply put, soon after VJ Day, a cadre of chaos resolvers representing both government and non-government agencies declared war on chaos. Actually, chaos is defined as complete confusion and disorder: a state in which behavior and events are not controlled by anything. Although the post-War era witnessed a great deal of confusion and disorder, human behavior and the events that resulted from it were controlled by a cacophony of forces and competing needs, some benign and some malevolent. Those who desired to force a modicum of order on the scene set out, with stout hearts and limited resources, to deal as best they could with a world where calamity appeared to reign supreme. These dedicated men and women struggled desperately to shift the pursuit of dispute resolution beyond the restrictive domain of abstract policy into the realm of concrete actions. In this, they echoed Descartes imperative to unlock the secrets hidden within all fields of human knowledge to bring order out of chaos; light out of darkness.

These missionaries of "Atomic Age" chaos resolution needed a powerful new tool that could be used with confidence to neutralize the spirit of non-cooperation that represented such a huge part of daily life in war-torn Europe and elsewhere. They heard about Game Theory's trustworthy and mathematically-provable models. They sought out the discipline's growing set of transferrable insights. They grappled with the concept of analogous predictive analytical modeling in an effort to wring some amount of certainty and order out of the turmoil encountered in their daily work. Their present-day descendants are still attempting to understand Game Theory's modeling and use it in that very same way.

'ANALOGOUS PREDICTIVE ANALYSIS', AND 'BRINKMANSHIP'

"We hear the Secretary of State boasting of his brinkmanship – the art of bringing us to the edge of the abyss."
-Adlai Stevenson

During the era of the Cold War (1947-1991), leaders in the United States and its allies and in the Soviet Union and its satellites played hand after hand of a terrifying little game known as 'Brinkmanship' (e.g. the Cuban Missile Crisis is one of the game's more famous hands). Here are the rules that govern this frightful game. To attain one's national policy goals, the rules of Brinkmanship require a player (Superpower "A") to employ a strategy of ever-escalating threats against his opponent. These threats are clearly perceived by the other player (Superpower "B") as hostile. This second player responds in his turn and escalates his own threats against his opponent. And so it goes.

SECTION 106 AND GAME THEORY

Imagine two irate fourth graders in a recess-filled schoolyard sideling around each other with teeth bared and big rocks in their hands, yelling with ever-increasing vehemence their threats of death and destruction at one another. Except in the case of Brinkmanship, the big rocks are hydrogen bombs.

The origin of the word 'Brinkmanship' has been attributed to Adlai Stevenson in his criticism of the Eisenhower Administration's foreign policy; a policy that Stevenson described as "going to the brink" of catastrophic nuclear war. According to Stevenson and others, eventually the threats and counter-threats made by the two Superpowers might well become un-retractable (similar escalations of threats had taken that same deadly course in the past). One or the other Superpower would then "call the bluff" of his opponent. At that point, it was only chance that determined whether both sides would back down simultaneously and allow 'cooler heads' to prevail, or 'go over the brink' into nuclear war (Read or watch "The Guns of August" for the failed Brinkmanship that presaged World War I and remember that beyond a certain point, Game Theory has nothing to say about "games of chance".)

The constant threat that hung over our world during the Cold War was that one superpower or the other would make an un-retractable threat and the other side would be unable to respond in any way other than by "going over the brink." Adlai Stevenson knew in his bones the continuing escalation of threats of nuclear war by one superpower against the other, if carried to extreme, had an ominous and fatalistic likelihood of leading to total destruction (watch "The Bedford Incident" for a dramatization of Brinkmanship's catastrophic endgame set in a microcosm).

Author's Note - Those who lived during that period shared that calamitous possibility with everyone else as an un-relenting fact of life. When recounting the long and war-torn history of this planet, the decades of the Cold War will stand as the era with the greatest potential for cataclysmic destruction.

The eminent journalist and author, William L. Shirer, best expressed the spirit of the times. "In our new age of terrifying, lethal gadgets, which supplanted so swiftly the old one, the first great aggressive war, if it should come, will be launched by suicidal little madmen pressing an electronic button. Such a war will not last long and none will ever follow it. There will be no conquerors and no conquests, but only the charred bones of the dead on an uninhabited planet." (The Rise and Fall of the Third Reich: A History of Nazi Germany, Simon & Schuster, 1960)

T. C. Schelling and the 'Real World'

With the Cold War as his context, Dr. Thomas C. Schelling's books, *The Strategy of Conflict*, (Harvard University Press, 1960) (Harvard University Press; Reprint edition (May 15, 1981)) and *Arms and Influence*, (Yale University Press, 1966) (Praeger; Reprint edition (February 18, 1977)) brought many of Game Theory's lessons, learned through the modeling of one-and-two-person board and card games, into the real and dangerous worlds of strategic theory and nuclear weapons policy. According to one reviewer on the book's Amazon.com website, (P.C., on September 7, 2006), "Before Schelling, Game Theory analysis was abstract and mathematical." It focused on zero-sum games, "where interests were purely conflicting and there were no incentives to cooperate." By contrast, Schelling's *The Strategy of Conflict* focused on real life examples and analyzed 'low-stakes' games that were analogous and therefore relevant to the 'high stakes' games he and his contemporaries encountered in their daily lives.

In *The Strategy of Conflict*, Schelling generalized existing Game Theory analysis of certain simple two-player games into more 'high-stakes' games that are played in the real world. Schelling described a number of recognized Game Theory-derived simple game strategies and then speculated about their application in matters of national security policy. In so doing, he offered example after example of real life bargaining in which each of the two players, if they were and remained rational, would rather make a concession than fail to reach any agreement at all. Schelling also emphasized that even in the game of Brinkmanship, there existed a wide range of outcomes that would be preferable to both players than no agreement at all, (Watch "The Missiles of October" or "Thirteen Days" for dramatizations of the successful game play that averted the Cuban Missile Crisis.).

In a July 28, 2013 article in Symposium Magazine entitled "Game Theory Is Useful, Except When It Is Not," Ariel D. Procaccia recounts one of Game Theory's most famous analogous test cases in which Schelling's 'real world' generalizations proved most useful. It occurred at the height of the Cold War.

"It is well-known that game theory informed U.S. nuclear strategy, and indeed, the interaction between the two opposing sides — NATO and the Warsaw Pact — can be modeled as the [ ] game, which is a variation of the famous "Prisoner's Dilemma."

Schelling's Game Theory generalizations in this case eventuated in the strategy of 'Mutually Assured Destruction' (MAD), where both the Soviet Union and the U. S. assembled hugh arsenals of hydrogen weapons. By 1970, the U. S. had amassed approximately 4,300 *million* tons of TNT equivalent nuclear bomb capacity and the Soviet Union had amassed approximately 3,100 *million* tons. This amassing of mega tonnage of nuclear destruction had risen to a point at which any actual use by one side would automatically result in full-scale nuclear war and the complete annihilation of both sides (Watch "Dr. Strangelove or: How I Learned to Stop Worrying and Love the Bomb" for a gallows humor dramatization of this scenario). The MAD-induced state of apocalypse guaranteed that no rational side *could* afford to attack the other. That meant that neither rational side would escalate the threat until it reached the point where it went "over the brink".

Author's Note – MAD brought both superpowers into a state of Nash Equilibrium (see 'Nash Equilibrium' below) that precluded any kind of endgame other than mutual annihilation, thus stalemating both rational sides against any further escalation). We can therefore take note of at least one instance of a positive Nash Equilibrium stalemate.

Author's Note – Of course, as any Game Theory adherent would readily admit, both sides in such a situation *must* be rational players. However, anyone who lived through the Cold War era will testify that there were times when we were not all that sure of the rationality of the players on either side; players who had their trigger fingers poised over 'the button'.

Author's Note – Recent incidents of harassment of U. S. armed forces patrol plans operating in international air space by the Russian military lead one to conclude that our world is fast approaching Round Two of Brinkmanship.

The fundamental Game Theory doctrine of analogous predictive analysis that lies at the heart of modern Game Theory and its usefulness as a powerful tool for the prevention and resolution of conflict in 'high stakes' games such as Brinkmanship owes a great debt to T. C. Schelling. Since the 1970s, Game Theorists like Schelling have been offering the rest of us the use of a mathematically provable set of rules that divide the universe of rational human interactions into sets of analogous groupings based upon their similarity of object, sequence, type, number of players, goals, strategies, and so forth.

We now know that, once we have enough evidence to identify a 'high-stakes' game as analogous to a simple, 'low-stakes' game for which we currently have a fool-proof Game Theory derivation, we can use that model to 'change the game' of the 'high stakes' game, we hope for the better!

'ANALOGOUS PREDICTIVE ANALYSIS' IN MORE DETAIL

"If words are to enter men's minds and bear fruit, they must be the right words shaped cunningly to pass men's defenses and explode silently and effectually within their minds."
- J. B. Phillips

One of today's keenest evangelists for Game Theory and its practical uses, Dr. Arthur T. Benjamin, argues that *all* board games are based upon mathematical models of patterned moves. He reasons that these board games are, therefore, abundantly amenable to mathematical analysis. Like his analytical forebear Descartes, Professor Benjamin believes that one can confidently use mathematical analysis and its resulting winning strategies to make sure that success prevails in these types of games.

Like Dr. Benjamin, we are all aware that humble, low-stakes, two-player board games such as Checkers are usually played 'just for fun'. We are just as aware that games at the high end of the spectrum, such as armed conflict between two powerful alliances of nations, such as was the case during the Cold War, might be played in a manner quite analogous to Checkers (confrontational move followed by predictable counter-move), (read any good narrative of the siege of Riga during Napoleon's invasion of Russia in 1812 to learn just how predictable such moves and counter-moves can be in war). However, nothing about these latter sorts of warlike games is 'playful' in any way.

Throughout the sorry history of this planet, the payoffs in these sorts of high-stakes, conflict-ridden games have always been negative for the *losing side*. These negative payoffs have been simply colossal in terms of loss of life, property, and national treasure. Furthermore, with few exceptions, even the *winners* of history's armed conflicts have suffered sufficiently in loss of life, property, and treasure to turn victory into ashes in their mouths (see the British Empire following World Wat II).

Author's Note - The most familiar of these 'Pyrrhic Victories' is named after king Pyrrhus of Epirus, which was a geographical and historical region in southeastern Europe, now shared between Greece and Albania. Here, Pyrrhus' army suffered irreplaceable casualties while *defeating* the Romans at Heraclea in 280 BC and Asculum in 279 BC during the Pyrrhic War. King Pyrrhus never recovered from his victories and Epirus eventually became a Roman vassal state. The end of the Epiran phase of the struggle between Greece and Rome opened the way for Roman dominance over the city states of Magna Graecia and advanced the Roman consolidation of power in Italy greatly. Therefore, even in victory, the advantage to the winner in the null-set game that is war often amounts to so little as to be worthless (See the MAD strategy for details).

SECTION 106 AND GAME THEORY

Author's Note – Here are some additional Pyrrhic Victories to think about / Yamamoto's Attack on Pearl Harbor – Marlborough's Battle Of Malplaquet – Santa Anna's Battle Of The Alamo – Gage's Battle Of Bunker Hill

Responding to these historical truths, modern Game Theory offers the possibility of thrashing out trustworthy sets of *mutually-affected winning strategies*. This possibility, coupled with Game Theory's strong commitment to analogous predictive analysis modeling, has caused its principles to become critical elements in the training programs of professional peacemakers, envoys, and diplomatists from around the globe; programs that reinforce the basic precepts of conflict resolution and prevention.

IF-THEN STATEMENTS

"If the world were good for nothing else, [then] it is a fine subject for speculation."
- *William Hazlitt*

Those who practice modern Game Theory modeling often use one of its most basic analytical tools; the '**if-then statement**'. The '**if**' part of the statement, or the hypothesis, places a tentative condition, qualifier, or caveat on the '**then**' part of the statement; the conclusion. If the condition is false, then the conclusion will also be false. If the condition is true, then the conclusion will also be true.

EXAMPLE: A typical if-then statement relative to Section 106 review would be, "**If** consultative consensus determines that there is a Historic Property located within an Undertaking's Area of Potential Effects (APE), **then** the Agency Official must assess the potential of that

Undertaking to affect that Historic Property". Game Theory mathematicians would express this '**if-then** statement' algebraically in the following formula...

$$NREL \rightarrow AEA$$

...where 'NREL' = National Register eligibility, and 'AEA' = Adverse Effect Assessment.

By way of a mathematical proof in the preceding Section 106 review example, the opposite conditional statement would be, "**if** consultative consensus were to determine that there are no Historic Properties located within an Undertaking's APE, **then** the Agency Official would not be obliged to assess the potential of the Undertaking to affect Historic Properties." This, obviously, is a true proof, given the rules of Section 106 review codified at 36 CFR 800. Since this is a true proof, the formula it proves is also true.

In any '**If-then** statement', the hypothesis and conclusion can be exchanged.

EXAMPLE: "**If** the Agency Official must assess the potential of her Undertaking to affect a Historic Property, **then** consultative consensus must have determined that there is a Historic Property located within the Undertaking's Area of Potential Effects (APE)".

By way of a mathematical proof in the preceding Section 106 review example, the opposite conditional statement would be, "**if** the Agency Official is not obliged to assess the potential of her Undertaking to affect Historic Properties, **then** consultative consensus has determined that there are no Historic Properties located within the Undertaking's APE."

Such provisional and conditional '**If-then statements**' appear throughout the 36 CFR 800 Regulation, just as they do within the rules of most other games. For the ease of the reader, I have highlighted the '**if-then statements**' contained in this book just as I did in the example given above.

DOMINATED AND DOMINANT STRATEGIES

"Whoever said, 'It's not whether you win or lose that counts,' probably lost."
- *Martina Navratilova*

In his very handy primer, *The Joy of Game Theory*, Presh Talwalkar devotes a fair amount of space to a discussion of positive and negative strategies used by the players of various types of games. In any game, writes Talwalkar, the success or failure of a player's strategies obviously governs whether she will attain her goal of not. Anybody who has ever played a game repeatedly soon learns that some strategies are always better than are others. Over time, seasoned game players may even come to recognize that some moves will never win while others will always win. Game Theorists refer to these as 'dominated' (never win no matter what any other player does) and 'dominant' (always win no matter what any other player does) strategies.

Clearly, it is in the best interest of a player to recognize and thereafter always avoid 'dominated' strategies and recognize and attempt always to put forward 'dominant' strategies. In no case is this truer than in the Section 106 review game.

However, Section 106 review players should be aware that both 'dominated' and 'dominant' strategies are not always easy to identify in that game, and even if some strategies are recognizable as 'dominant', certain players, even rational ones, do not always use them. Even so, a portion of the remainder of this book will be devoted to identifying sets of 'dominated' and 'dominant' strategies used by players in the Section 106 review game.

WORDS

"I have hated words and I have loved them, and I hope I have made them right."
— *Markus Zusak*

Words have specific meaning depending upon the context in which they are said or spoken. The board and card games that Game Theorists subject to their mathematical modeling have words associated with them that have specific meanings based upon the context of the board games themselves. Here are some of the more important board game words.

1) Board — The game board upon which the game is played. In Section 106 review, the board is the figurative consultation table around which all participants sit.

2) Capture — A method for removing another player's game pieces from the game board that is compliant with the rules of that game. The example board game used in this book where capture is the object is NIM. Its pieces represent various stages in a specific Section 106 review.

3) Turn/Move — A player's opportunity within the rules of the game either to move a game piece or to make a 'bidding'

SECTION 106 AND GAME THEORY

decision. In Section 106 review, the Agency Official always makes the first move, and the State Historic Preservation Officer/Tribal Historic Preservation Officer (SHPO/THPO) and other participants move in turn in response.

4) Pass — A forfeiture of a turn by a player. If the SHPO does not respond to a formal submission by the Agency Official of her determinations and findings within the 30 days allowed by the rules of the game, the Agency Official may assume a pass and continue to the next round of the game.

5) Call — A player's formal settlement to end a round of game play through mutual agreement with the other player. The SHPO may 'call' the Agency Official's formal submission of determinations of findings by reaching consensus and so notifying the Agency Official.

6) Pie Rule — A rule, which, if agreed upon by both players, eliminates any advantage of moving first. After the first players' opening move, the second player has the option of swapping sides to take up where the first player left off. There is no Pie Rule in Section 106 review.

7) Rule — A condition, convention, or stipulation by which a game is played. The rules of Section 106 review are ordained by the NHPA and are separately codified at 36 CFR 800.

8) Ruleset — The comprehensive set of rules that define game play and govern a game. The ruleset for the game of Section 106 review is 36 CFR 800.

9) Best Play — The strategy (or strategies) which produces the most favorable outcome for a player, taking other players' strategies as a given. In Section 106 review best play eventuates in a common payoff beneficial to all participants.

GOALS AND STRATEGIES / UTILITY THEORY

"If you have many goals, and you don't reach your goals, it is very upsetting, so I just think of keeping it simple, working hard and going and playing the game."
- *Yuvraj Singh*

Within his or her particular set of participants, each rational, intelligent player with sufficient standing to enter a Section 106 review game will be expected to bring to the consultation table a pre-determined collection of payoff goals ('utilities') to be attained and an assortment of pre-determined strategies for attaining those goals.

Goals

Game Theory teaches that the selection of a player's 'utility' payoff (the highest possible value or the lowest possible risk) originates in that player's perceived ability to gain something out of the game to satisfy his needs or wants within the boundaries set by the game's rules. Therefore, the pre-game selection of the goals a player wishes to attain will begin with his appraisal of what it would take to satisfy his needs or wants. This selection will become more realistic as the player gains awareness of the limits imposed by the rules of the game.

Here is a list of the players in a Game of Section 106 review and a general statement of their needs. The Agency Official's 'needs' involve completion of the Section 106 review process as painlessly and as promptly as possible. The applicant for Federal assistance's 'needs' are the same. The SHPO/THPO's 'needs' involve identification, evaluation, and protection of Historic Properties. Tribal and Native Hawaiian Organizations' 'needs' involve the same. Representatives of Local Governments' 'needs' center around maintaining their municipal land use controls. Affected private property owners' 'needs' center around protecting their 'best use' interests. Heritage Stewardship organizations' 'needs' center around advocating for the protection of Historic Properties.

Strategies

Rational game players will begin game play with strategies they believe will attain their need-based goals. During game play, they will continually assess their own strategies as well as those of the players around them. They will determine strategies to be 'good' or 'bad' depending on the type of payoff each strategy has gained in the past for the player using it or for other players she has observed. Obviously, rational game players will favor 'good', 'most preferable', 'dominant' strategies over 'bad', 'least preferable', 'dominated' ones. However, Game Theorists readily acknowledge that not all players are rational (more about rational/honorable and irrational/dishonorable strategies later).

Goals and Strategies

If a selected strategy succeeds in attaining its assigned utility payoff goal, **then** the player attaining that goal has met his need and satisfied his desire. When a player attains a desired goal, he or she receives a reward of some sort corresponding to that goal. **If** a strategy does not succeed, **then** the player receives a punishment connected with the failure to meet his need. Game Theorists refer to both these rewards and punishments as 'payoffs'.

Therefore, payoffs can be either positive or negative, depending, as Dr. Stevens points out, on how much a player likes or dislikes the outcome of the game. This concept is important because it mirrors rationality. Stevens is correct to observe that neither the intrinsic value of a payoff nor the value placed upon it by other players is the final arbiter of its value to a rational player. To that player, the value of a payoff is measured solely by the amount of positive or negative reward it offers to the player evaluating it; how well it meets his needs. In Section 106 review, that which often appears to most players as a small payoff may actually bring great satisfaction and value to the player who attains it.

Ordering Goals and Strategies

Morton Davis reminds us that Game Theorists state as a matter of course that rational players will always base their pre-determined selection of strategies upon a clear understanding of the specific goals ('utilities') they wish to attain, knowing through past experience that certain strategies are better at achieving certain goals than are others. However, Game Theorists also understand that actually selecting that best set of goals and ordering them in correct line of preference is not as easy as it might seem. This is so because separating one's needs and wants into sets of "have-tos" and "wouldn't it be nice ifs" can be difficult, especially if there is a strong emotional component involved.

To make the selection and sorting of goals easier, Utility Theory, a kind of sub-set of Game Theory, proposes a collection of useful Cartesian axioms that players may use to sort and then rank a group of 'right' goals from among all goals that are attainable in a given instance assuming compliance with the rules of the game. These condition-setting

Cartesian axioms determine the hierarchy of goals that rational players will adopt. A comprehensive treatment of these axioms can be found at *Utility Theory For Decision Making* by Peter C. Fishburn, John Wiley & Sons, 1970.

Here are the Utility Theory axioms that seem most relevant to Section 106 review.

1) **goals and strategies are comparable** – When faced with two possible goals or strategies, a player should compare them one against the other and decide their relative appeal based solely upon his intuitive preference of one over the other (notice *intuitive* preference over logical, emotional, or experiential preference).

This is the 'better / worse' scenario used by optometrists when seeking patient input on the best lenses to prescribe. When stating which given lens is "better" or "worse", the eye exam patient is usually being guided by what can only be described as "a feeling in my bones". Anyone who has ever gone through this selection process will readily admit that it calls for split-second responses that haven't the luxury of the deliberate analysis required by either logic, emotion, or experience.

However, In Section 106 review, just as in optometry, what may seem a 'better' choice at first blush might not ultimately turn out to be so.

EXAMPLE: Let's suppose an applicant for Federal assistance is unfamiliar with Section 106 review's rules that require consultative consensus between the Agency Official/applicant and the SHPO concerning the National Register eligibility of Cultural Resources located within an Undertaking's Area of Potential Effects. Furthermore, this applicant is completely unaware of the SHPO's standing goal of identifying any Historic Properties that may be located inside each applicant's project impact area. Unlike the SHPO, who sees identification of Historic Properties as one of the principal goals of Section 106 consultation, this applicant sees no value whatsoever in Historic Properties. Therefore,

SECTION 106 AND GAME THEORY

when presented with what, to him, appears to be a simple and logical, either/or choice between determining that there are Historic Properties inside his impact area and determining that there are no Historic Properties, he immediately determines that none exists, shunning the regulatory requirement for supplying corroborative evidence of that fact to the SHPO.

He does this because, having miss-read the rules of the game, he naively believes he is free to make this determination all on his own. He thinks his determination will allow him quickly to retire from the game and attain his true goal of moving ahead with his Undertaking unhindered. He thinks he has cleverly avoided what he views as an un-necessary hardship; the requirement of devoting the valuable time, money, and effort required actually to identify Historic Properties within his impact area. However, far from being a benefit, his miss-reading of the rules will lead to costly and risky consequences.

This somewhat (only somewhat) exaggerated example demonstrates the importance of becoming familiar with the rules of a game such as Section 106 review before trying to attain goals that are possibly unattainable.

2) **goals and strategies are transitive** – When faced with three possible attainable goals ('A', 'B', and 'C'), a player can still estimate their relative desirability if she groups them into *two pairs*. **If** the player likes goal 'A' more than goal 'B' in the first pair, and goal 'B' more than goal 'C' in the second pair, **then** she does not need to waste time comparing goal 'A' and goal 'C', because it is a Cartesian certainty she will like goal 'C' least of all.

EXAMPLE: An SHPO may compare a Federal Agency Official's avoidance alternative 'A' against her minimization alternative 'B' and prefer the avoidance alternative over the minimization alternative (the preparation of an historic resources management plan that will require the screening of the Undertaking from the Historic Property). Then he may compare her minimization alternative 'B' against her mitigation alternative 'C' stipulated in a draft Memorandum of Agreement and prefer the minimization one over the mitigated one. He will **then** prefer the presented alternatives in the following utility rank order: avoidance, minimization, mitigation, and therefore has no need to compare "A" and "C".

3) **indifference to payoffs translates into indifference to the rules of the game**.

If none of the allowable payoffs at the end of a Section 106 review game appeals to a particular player, **then** she will most likely become indifferent to playing by the rules of the game. This is also true **if** all of the possible payoffs conflict with her own hoped-for goals. **Then**, she may even retire from the game altogether.

EXAMPLE: Certain participants in a Section 106 review cooperate to voice a strong preference for an alternative that would completely avoid adverse effect to an identified Historic Property over another, agency-preferred alternative that would surely result in adverse effect. The Agency Official, wedded to her original, impactful, preferred alternative, has no interest in any payoff that might result from changing her mind and adopting the other players' suggested alternative. Therefore, she may react to their proposal by trying to 'bend' the rules of the game. Perhaps, out of her desire to move the others to abandon their own preferences, she may even try to apply political or some other type of pressure against the other players so that she might attain her ultimate goal of getting on with her preferred alternative unobstructed.

4) **a player will gamble when tempted by good odds of achieving a desired goal**. However, the level at which he is willing to gamble is equal to the relative 'goodness' of the odds (See the section on 'Prospect Theory' below.).

EXAMPLE: **If** an SHPO has good reason to gamble that Historic Properties of much greater significance will eventually be avoided by the Agency Official's modified Undertaking, **then** he will remain in a Section 106 review game for a long period of time and may even compromise on the loss of integrity of some less significant Historic Properties.

5) **a player will stay in a game with multiple rounds only so long as he feels that the ultimate payoff will attain his desired goal and that the corresponding reward is truly valuable**.

EXAMPLE: **If** a County Historian believes he has reliable evidence that by doing so he will eventually prevail upon the Agency Official to avoid adversely affecting the county's most significant Historic Property**,** **then** he will suffer through the tedium of multiple Formal Consulting Party Meetings.

JAKE NIELSON AND DOMINANT GOALS

Jake Nielson ("The Basics of Game Theory: Dominant Strategies and Nash Equilibrium" (The Innovative Manager website, posted November 25, 2014)) maintains that most people in the field of dispute resolution who use Game Theory's lessons are not equipped, either by training or intellectual capacity, to derive the Game Theory calculations that prove the validity of those lessons. His conclusion is that they do not need to do what Game Theorists do to understand and use Game Theory's lessons.

Nielson states that, at base, Game Theory is about analyzing certain player decisions that will influence other players' decisions. Game Theorists refer to these types of decisions as 'strategies.' His article offers a simple checklist for ascertaining the best, 'dominant' strategies players may use in a given game.

Using Nielson as a model, I propose that Game Theory is also about analyzing a player's *goals* that will influence other players' goals. As we have already seen, the simple idea behind Utility Theory is that one *can* calculate what is the right goal to attain even in multi-player games, even before needing to declare it at the consultation table. This being the case, I am going to use Nielson's simple checklist for determining Dominant Strategies to determine a set of Section 106 review's Dominant Goals. Here is Nielson's simple checklist:

Step 1: Define the Players

In every game, there must be players. Therefore, the first step to constructing a Game Theory analysis is to identify all the players involved. Nielson recommends that it is best to keep the number of players down to two, if possible, since the vast majority of Game Theory's derivations are for two-person games. Adding more players than two complicates matters greatly. If the game does have more than two players, Nielson suggests it is best to group them into two broad sets with similar strategies. Here, I am substituting goals for strategies.

In Section 106 review, there are usually two inclusive sets of players that act in concert as participants; the Pro-Undertaking Set and the Pro-Protection Set.

The Pro-Undertaking Set

1. Agency Officials
2. Applicants for Federal assistance

3. Groups with standing because of a demonstrated interest in the Undertaking due to the nature of their legal or economic relation to the Undertaking or affected properties

The Pro-Protection Set

1. ACHP
2. THPOs
3. Tribal Representatives
4. Groups with standing because of a demonstrated interest in the Undertaking due to the nature of their concern with the Undertaking's effects on Historic Properties

In addition, there is an **Independent Set** comprised of Representatives of Local Government and Private Property Owners whose interests lie with one or the other of the major groups depending upon the particular case under review. Finally, there is the **Umpire** in the person of the SHPO, charged with certifying compliance with the rules of the game by assisting and advising the Agency Official and other participants.

Step 2: List the Possible Goals Available to Each Player

According to Utility Theory, each player has a pre-identified list of available goals. In Section 106 review, the *complete* list of possible goals is the same for each of the four sets.

1. No Cultural Resources Affected
2. No Historic Properties Affected
3. Historic Properties Affected
4. No Adverse Effect
5. Conditional No Adverse Effect
6. Avoided Adverse Effect
7. Minimized Adverse Effect
8. Mitigated Adverse Effect

Step 3: Create a Scenarios Matrix

A scenarios matrix shows the players and the list of goals available to them in a matrix format. The cells inside the matrix represent the specific scenarios that can play out. To set up a scenarios matrix, one simply takes the Sets and the goals available to each Set and lists them in a table (more about Scenario Matrices later).

Step 4: List How Much Each Player Values Each Goal in a Payoff Matrix

Nielson states that this is the most difficult part of the checklist to fulfill properly. He is correct because so much of the assignment of value points that give weight to each strategy or payoff goal is subjective to the player ascribing weight to it. Therefore, I am only going to attempt it for the Pro-Undertaking Set and the Pro-Protection Set. I have subjectively assigned point weights to the goals listed for each Set based upon my years of experience in the field. Some of the point valuations are obvious, while others may surprise readers unfamiliar with the process. All point weights are the result of my best effort to assign goal points based upon

SECTION 106 AND GAME THEORY

my understanding of the relative values each Set has placed on various goals based upon either highest value or lowest risk.

Pro-Undertaking Set

Agency Officials
Applicants for Federal assistance
Groups with standing because of a demonstrated interest in the Undertaking due to the nature of their legal or economic relation to the Undertaking or affected properties

Goals in order of assigned value:

No Cultural Resources Identified – *14 points / dominant goal*
No Historic Properties Affected – 12 points
Historic Properties Affected – 3 points
No Adverse Effect – 10 points
Conditional No Adverse Effect – 8 points
Avoided Adverse Effect – 6 points
Minimized Adverse Effect – 4 points
Mitigated Adverse Effect – *1 point / dominated goal*

Pro-Protection Set

ACHP
THPOs
Tribal Representatives
Groups with standing because of a demonstrated interest in the Undertaking due to the nature of their concern with the Undertaking's effects on Historic Properties

Goals in order of assigned value:

No Cultural Resources Identified – 8 points
No Historic Properties Affected – 10 points
Historic Properties Affected - 4 points
No Adverse Effect – *12 points / dominant goal*
Conditional No Adverse Effect – 9 points
Avoided Adverse Effect – 6 points
Minimized Adverse Effect – 4 points
Mitigated Adverse Effect – *1 point / dominated goal*

Step 5: Look For Dominant Goals (and Dominated Goals as well)

A 'dominant' goal is one that is preferable for one player no matter what any other player seeks to attain. For the Pro-Undertaking Set, the dominant goal will eventuate in a payoff of no Cultural Resources Identified because it affords the least risk and the speediest conclusion of the game. For the Pro-Protection Set, the dominant goal will eventuate in a payoff of No Adverse Effect to a Historic Property because it identifies and evaluates a Historic Property perhaps previously unidentified while posing the least risk to it.

As an aside, in Game Theory, a 'dominated' goal is one that is least preferable for one player no matter what any other player seeks to obtain. For the Pro-Undertaking Set, the dominated goal will eventuate in a payoff of Mitigated Adverse Effect because of the added risk to the Undertaking posed by the extra time, effort, and expense of mitigating the adverse effect. The same holds true for the Pro-Protection Set because of the high risk to the identified Historic Property posed by the adverse effect that must be mitigated.

The fact that both sides will have the same dominated goal of a mitigated adverse effect should encourage them both to take whatever steps are necessary to avoid it.

GOALS AND STRATEGIES / PROSPECT THEORY

As I grow older, I pay less attention to what men say. I just watch what they do."
- Andrew Carnegie

If a player has been diligent in her use of the appropriate theorems and 'conditions' offered by Utility Theory, once she selects her goals and ranks them in order of desirability, **then** those goals and their order of preference should remain pretty much the same throughout the game. This is the crux of Utility Theory. Prospect Theorists disagree.

Prospect Theorists point out that, for there to be 'Perfect Play' in Utility Theory controlled games, each rational player must believe that her selected strategy will always lead to her best possible outcome while *not taking into account* the response by the other players. Any experience at all in playing games will confirm that the responses of players during game play can be counted upon to require the other players to modify their strategies. For them, 'Perfect Play' requires a player's strategy to lead to the best possible outcome for that player *regardless* of the response by her opponents.

According to Morton Davis, 'Prospect Theory' or 'Loss-Aversion Theory' is a sort of subset of Game Theory that takes a more nuanced view of the way in which players set and keep hold of their goals during game play than does Utility Theory. Unlike those created by Utility Theory, Prospect Theory's mathematical formulas predict the responses of game players based upon the 'prospect' of how the outcome of the game is presented to them at a particular point during play, and, to an extent, who it is who presents that outcome to them. Prospect Theory was first developed by Daniel Kahneman and Amos Tversky in 1979. Kahneman is professor emeritus of psychology and public affairs at Princeton University's Woodrow Wilson School and recipient of the 2002 Nobel Memorial Prize in Economic Sciences (shared with Vernon L. Smith). Tversky (March 16, 1937 – June 2, 1996) was a major collaborator with Daniel Kahneman, and a key figure in the discovery of systematic human cognitive bias and handling of risk.

Prospect Theory suggests that a player assigns value to perceived possible *gains* over time differently from the way in which she assigns value to perceived possible *losses*. Therefore, as game play continues, a player will be more willing to gamble (to risk loss) after each re-assessment of her perceived short-term gains while less willing to gamble after a re-assessment of her perceived short-term losses.

1) **If** a player is offered the choice of two end-game payoffs of exactly equal positive value, one expressed only in terms of a series of short-term gains moving toward that payoff and the other in terms of a series of short-term alternating gains and losses, but still ending in that same payoff, **then** she will almost always choose the former scenario. In doing so, she is following simple, intuitive rules that influence her judgments and, according to Prospect Theory, these intuitive rules practically make her decisions for her. These intuitive rules reflect mental shortcuts that channel the brain into focusing on one part

of a complex problem to the exclusion of all others. Typically, these intuitions grow out of '**availability**' or the ease with which a particular idea can be brought readily to mind, and '**representativeness**' as seen when people allow pre-judged stereotyping categories or pigeonholing to sway their decision making.

- **Availability / EXAMPLE**: **If** visions of strawberry ice cream waft frequently through a player's brain, **then** she will be likely to view a bowl of strawberry ice cream set before her as more desirable than she would a bowl of chocolate ice cream, even if, on other occasions, she would say she likes chocolate better than strawberry.

EXAMPLE: **If** references to a specific Historic Property recur constantly within a Section 106 review during the course of a game, **then** a Consulting Party will be more likely to consider an Undertaking that completely avoids that Historic Property as preferable to one that merely minimizes project-related effect to that property. This will be true even if his preferred Undertaking would adversely affect another Historic Property about which he has not been constantly reminded.

- **Representativeness / EXAMPLE: If** a player is trying to decide whether a met-for-the-first-time fellow player is a 'good guy' or a 'bad guy', **then** he will try to spot a specific identifying characteristic connected with that player. He will feel a raised level of influence **if** the assessed player's identifying characteristic is very similar to a prototype he already has firmly in his mind.

EXAMPLE: **If** a Consulting Party had encountered a very tall robber at some time in his past, **then** he might well be more likely to view a tall Agency Official as a potential 'robber'. Similarly, **if** an Agency Official has suffered through past bouts of continuous argument with the

SHPO of a certain state, **then** she is more likely to view all SHPOs as 'the enemy' and act intuitively upon that perception.

2) **If**, during the course of a game, a player detects a highly prized reward lodged within a (to her) valuable payoff at the end of a game, **then** she is more likely to risk loss during successive rounds of the same game in hopes of attaining that much-prized end-game payoff.

EXAMPLE: **If** The President of a Historic District Neighborhood Association receives long-term assurances from the Agency Official that she will stipulate in a Memorandum of Agreement that she will press for no further encroachments in a historic district for a period of ten years, **then** he will be more willing to risk the loss of a small corner of that historic district to the Undertaking under review.

3) A player will tend to de-value outcomes seen as a mixed bag of gains and losses and seek instead un-nuanced resolutions that focus on outcomes of clear gain or loss.

EXAMPLE: **If** an Agency Official is faced with the option of carrying out her Undertaking as intended but with the added costs of screening the project from the Historic Property and she is aware that screening would indeed minimize project-related effects upon a Historic Property yet add significantly to the total project cost, **then** she might choose to abandon the Undertaking altogether and console herself that she really did not wish to carry it out anyway (See the Aesop's Fable of the Sour Grapes.).

Prospect Theory argues that those pre-determined goals and the pre-determined strategies for attaining them that a rational and perceptive player brings to the game are very likely to change during the course of play because of that player's interaction with other players. Furthermore, the original rank order of that player's goals and strategies

SECTION 106 AND GAME THEORY

may also change. Therefore, Prospect Theory makes constant demands upon players to stay alert to changing patterns among other players who continue to interact throughout the course of game play. As Professor Ridgley makes clear in his treatment of Game Theory, its principles urge game participants constantly to re-assess not only their own goals and strategies but those of the other players as well. Ridgley stresses the concept that the responses of players to the 'plays' of other participants as the game continues assist all participants in re-identifying their current best strategies for achieving highest payoffs.

EXAMPLE: A young woman wakes up one Saturday morning to discover that she really wants to own a nice shiny new blue bicycle today (her pre-determined goal). As she reads the morning newspaper, she sees a store's advertisement for bicycles. In the ad, the bicycles all cost the same amount of money. The only apparent difference among them is in the color; some red, some yellow, and some blue. By using the 'transitive pairs' approach suggested by Utility Theory, the young woman confirms her preference for the blue version over the others (her first Utility Theory goal) and immediately heads off to the bike shop to buy a blue bicycle today (her first Utility Theory strategy).

If, as she walks into the store, however, she sees a big sign that announces "30% off on all red bicycles bought today", **then**, she must re-evaluate her pre-determined and modified rank order of desirability based purely upon color preference in light of her new interaction with the owner of the bike shop who is offering the discount. Now, she shifts from wanting a blue bicycle at full price to wanting a red one (her second color choice) at 30% off (her first Prospect Theory modified goal), but she still wants to buy it today at 30% off (her first Prospect Theory modified strategy). However, **if** she sees a second sign that reads, "An additional 30% off on all red bicycles purchased one week from today", **then** she may decide to defer her purchase of a red bicycle until next week (her second Prospect Theory modified goal) and give up entirely on her original goal of purchasing a brand new blue bicycle today (her second Prospect Theory modified strategy).

As players interact with the other participants while the game progresses, those players in a game of Section 106 review who began with pre-defined sets of ordered goals and strategies in mind might well find themselves in a similar situation as is our bike purchaser.

Summary

Professor Ridgley emphasizes the notion that "the ability to *change* the play – or the game plan – is what distinguishes genuine strategy". Professor Benjamin would certainly agree. He argues that players in a game such as Section 106 review should take the time beforehand to identify and order their goals, and then select a promising opening strategy, and then be prepared to vary that strategy, and perhaps even the goals that dictated it, in reaction to the moves of the other players to remain flexible. This flexible, interdependent course of action offers the best possibility of successful completion of the review process.

RATIONAL/HONORABLE AND IRRATIONAL/DISHONORABLE GAME STRATEGIES

"Be true to the game, because the game will be true to you. If you try to shortcut the game, then the game will shortcut you."
- *Michael Jordan*

The reason Game Theory's lessons are useful in Section 106 review is that almost all that game's players are rational. As such, they bring to the table a collection of discerning, pre-determined strategies designed to help attain whatever rational goals they have set for themselves. However, just as in any other 'game of chance', Section 106 review also acquires some irrational players who might well be tempted to use dishonorable strategies to attain their own goals.

Among the most obvious dishonorable strategies they may employ are:
1) resorting to rhetorical tricks as an appeal to human emotion against fact and reason
2) using fallacious arguments in an attempt to deflect attention from the real issues being discussed
3) delaying any final decision-making merely for the sake of delay, and
4) faking evidence to support an irrational player's position

At times, even the most adroitly facilitated consultation whose goal is dispute resolution may be plagued by clashes among its participants. Often, these clashes result from a biased participant's calculated and purposeful introduction of one or the other of those dishonorable strategies into the discussion with the express purpose of interfering with the smooth resolution of contentious or disputatious issues.

Whenever participants in facilitated Section 106 consultations resort to dishonorable strategies to buttress their assertions, the SHPO's representative has a responsibility to challenge those participants and to keep the consultation relevant and productive for everyone concerned. Specifically, SHPO representatives should insist that an Agency Official, applicant, or other Consulting Party provide demonstrable logical or empirical causal evidence to support any assertion made during a Formal Consulting Parties Meeting. Furthermore, SHPO representatives should emphasize that, in place of these dishonorable strategies, the game of Section 106 review offers its players an authorized assortment of rational and honorable strategies all participants may use with confidence to further the achievement of their goals. Honorable Section 106 review strategies include:

1) emphasizing relevant facts in support of the player's own determinations and findings
2) emphasizing errors or omissions in another player's determinations and findings
3) emphasizing completeness and accuracy in the player's own supporting documents
4) emphasizing errors, omissions, or inconsistencies in another player's supporting documentation, and
5) bluffing for strategic reasons (Yes, this is an honorable strategy. More later)

Keep in mind that one player's 'facts' may appear to be another player's 'fallacy'. Therefore, a Section 106 review participant should be ready to test the intellectual honesty of the other players in the game as they present what they claim to be a set of 'facts' to support their positions. At his website, Mike Gene, an astute student of fair play in

SECTION 106 AND GAME THEORY

games, has collected a useful list of ten signs of intellectual honesty among players.

Honest Players:

1) do not overstate the power of their own argument
2) are willing publicly to acknowledge that reasonable alternative viewpoints exist
3) are willing publicly to acknowledge and question their own assumptions and biases
4) are willing publicly to acknowledge where their argument is weak
5) are willing publicly to acknowledge when they are wrong
6) demonstrate consistency in their statements
7) address the argument instead of attacking the person making the argument
8) do not misrepresent an argument, either their own or another 'player's
9) demonstrate a commitment to critical thinking
10) are willing publicly to acknowledge when a criticism of their argument is valid

If a player exhibits these traits while consulting with other players during a Section 106 review game, **then** chances are quite good that all other players will have reason to trust the honesty of her determinations and findings and the rational strategies she employs to support them.

There are a number of sound techniques available for dealing with participants who attempt to use dishonorable strategies during the Section 106 review game. The best technique is, first to sympathize with the person using the dishonorable strategy, then to request that the person provide the tests, proofs, and data that will support the assertion made by the use of that strategy. Usually, when pressed, the person making the dishonorable assertion will modify it to a more reasonable assertion or retract it altogether, and the consultation can get back on track. **If** this technique does not succeed, and the person persists with the dishonorable strategy, **then** the SHPO representative should call for a break in the consultation and have a quiet heart to heart talk with the person and inform him or her that the assertion will be tabled in the discussion until and unless the person making it can bring sufficient proof and evidentiary data to the discussion to support the assertion.

MAXIMS

"Even hackneyed and commonplace maxims are to be used, if they suit one's purpose."
- *Aristotle*

A maxim is a short, pithy statement expressing a general truth. By using the game-defining maxims proposed by Game Theorists that combine the goal-defining and ordering theorems proposed by Utility Theorists and the strategic cautions of the Prospect Theorists, rational and intelligent players should be able to:

1) compare, rank, select, and communicate their pre-determined goals before play begins
2) adopt honorable strategies for achieving their goals
3) adapt their original goals and strategies based upon interdependent interactions with other players as play moves along from one round to the next
4) cooperate with other players to attain binding agreements that reflect positive payoffs

SECTION 106 AND GAME THEORY

Participants in Section 106 review must keep in mind the following prime maxims of Game Theory. These prime maxims are those agreed upon by the various authorities on Game Theory I have studied.

5) *each player will make decisions in agreement with his own wishes.* **If** the game is to be successful, **then** each of the *other* players must take those decisions into account as they further their own goals.

   This maxim agrees perfectly with Section 106 review's flexible and continual interdependent consultation that allows a player to be aware of the decisions of the others and take them into account.

6) *each player must communicate openly with the other players.* **If** this open communication does not occur, **then** the game fails.

   Open, honest, and rational consultation is indispensable to successful Section 106 review.

7) *each player must determine whether his goals agree with or clash with those of other players.*

   By doing so, certain Section 106 review participants may be persuaded to form cooperative alliances that support the Agency Official's determinations and findings while others may decide that their goals are better served by forming alliances that challenge those same determinations and findings.

8) *each player must decide at any given point in game play whether to cooperate or compete with other players.*

   During a game of Section 106 review, this decision will reflect each player's opinions concerning shared or competing goals.

SECTION 106 AND GAME THEORY

9) *each player must play strictly by the cooperative rules of the game.* **If** a player does not do so, **then** he must retire from play and seek resolution elsewhere.

>Section 106 review is not confrontational or litigious by design. Its rules assume cooperation among the players rather than confrontation. Therefore, any player wishing to resort to litigious strategies should resign from Section 106 review and find other games to play. Such are certainly available and easily discovered. The most obvious is called "Federal District Court Lawsuit".

10) *each player may seek to secure certain rewarding payoffs through a 'binding agreement' with the other players.*

>Mutually-agreed-upon "No Adverse Effect" conditions or "Resolution of Adverse Effect" stipulations contained within mitigated agreement documents of one sort or another are Section 106 review's best means of making sure of a proper resolution of project-related effects and a successful end game.

11) *each player will use the game to manipulate circumstances while in full knowledge that circumstances are manipulating him at the same time.*

>The consultative give and take passed among the participants so essential to the doctrine of Prospect Theory is vital to properly conducted Section 106 reviews.

12) *each player will find a game to be increasingly resistant to Game Theory's predictive modeling as it 1) becomes more nuanced; 2) absorbs increasing amounts of time and effort; 3) increases risk.*

>Such is the case with a Section 106 review that generates additional Cultural Resources surveys, reports, site visits,

or Formal Consulting Party Meetings, gains additional players, or becomes subject to irrational play.

13) ironically, **if** *a game that is long and drawn out still remains stable throughout,* **then** *each player will find it to be increasingly unrewarding to his or her ego.* Nobody likes a tie game and everybody wants to be a "rainmaker".

Section 106 reviews of long duration that remain compliant and produce evenhanded outcomes are not particularly ego rewarding, even though they certainly do offer participants attractive payoffs in the end.

INDUCEMENTS AND RESTRICTIONS

"Without deadlines and restrictions I just tend
to become preoccupied with other things."
- *Val Kilmer*

In any type of game, an assortment of inducements prompts a player to remain in the game while a host of restrictions prevents that player from going outside the rules of the game to win.

Inducements

Section 106 review is a special case because, it is the participatory requirement of the game itself rather than any promise of positive payoffs that supplies the primary inducement for joining in and remaining in the game. That primary inducement is obviously supplied by the statutory and regulatory requirement that Agency Officials. SHPOs, THPOs, Tribal Representatives, and a host of other participants *must* seek each other out and continue to consult until resolution has been reached. Nevertheless, common sense dictates that, other than this key regulatory constraint, an important inducement to remaining in a game of sequence such as Section 106 review must be the promise of an eventual positive payoff.

However, this is by no means Section 106 review's only inducement. Within the past forty years, Game Theorists have presented solid mathematical evidence proving that the extent to which the rules of a game allow and even encourage players to communicate with each other during the course of play is directly proportional to their willingness to stay in the game in expectation that they will attain their goals eventually. Cross-communication among participants runs through the entire Section 106 review process.

Prospect Theory enlarges upon this evidence by stating that interdependent communication among the participants during game play allows them access to both the opportunity and the encouragement to modify their strategies and goals, either to align them more closely with those of other players through cooperation or to challenge the goals and strategies of other players through competition. Cross-communication helps players as they decide whether to compete or cooperate during a specific round of review based upon their own mutable goals.

Restrictions

Here is a collection of restrictions associated with Section 106 review that either incite players to retire from the game prematurely or induce them into remaining at the table until the final showdown.

> 1) **the restrictions** imposed by 36 CFR 800 have both positive and negative consequences because a positive

SECTION 106 AND GAME THEORY

consequence for one player might translate into a negative consequence for another. Continuous, interdependent consultation is supposed to counteract this 'null set' aspect of the game, and usually it does.

2) **the mandated order of play** in Section 106 review has both positive and negative consequences. At times, the early bird who chooses to concatenate compatible Steps in the process catches the worm of successful and prompt completion; at other times, a too-early worm who pre-decides her determinations and findings without benefit of consultation is caught in the trap of non-compliant foreclosure of opportunity to comment.

3) **a threat** made by a participant against other players is effective only **if** it is plausible. The more there is obvious risk in terms of cost in time and money that is associated with carrying out a threat, the less plausible it is.

4) effective and truly binding **endgame agreements** reached through consensus among the players must contain provisions for monitoring and **commitment tracking** to be plausible.

Even so, we know that all the cooperative consultation that has led to consensus in the first place and all the mutually-agreed-to mechanisms of enforcement carried in the agreement document do not necessarily ensure that it will succeed in resolving conflict.

SECTION 106 AND GAME THEORY

THE INFLUENCE OF 'COMMON KNOWLEDGE'

"Journeys end in lovers meeting. Every wise man's son doth know."
— William Shakespeare

Common knowledge is knowledge that is known by everyone or nearly everyone, usually with reference to the specific community to which the term is applied. In a community that identifies itself as a set of players of a specific game, common knowledge is comprised of the knowledge about permissible game play mutually adopted by that community.

Example: Everyone who ever played Monopoly as a child knows that there is the printed booklet of Monopoly rules, and then there is "Neighborhood Monopoly" that has its own mutually-agreed-to ruleset that is common knowledge among the neighborhood kids.

According to Professor Scott Stevens, most disciples of Game Theory assume a state of common knowledge among the players, just as assuredly as they assume that players are rational. Professor Stevens defines a piece of 'common knowledge as a "bit of information known by all players who know all players know it". **Example:** In Section 106 review, for instance, it is common knowledge that the Agency Official must consult with the appropriate SHPO, or THPO, or other Consulting Parties as she formulates her determinations and findings. This bit of common knowledge comes from the official ruleset of 36 CFR 800. Another bit of common knowledge has to do with 'eligibility' for listing in the National Register of Historic Places being the instigator for an Agency Official's assessment of project-related effects, and not National Register 'listing', per se. This too is a bit of common knowledge derived from the formal Section 106 review ruleset. However, each SHPO has her own mutually-agreed-to ruleset that I shall refer to as "Neighborhood 106" derived through years of consultation with Agency Officials and applicants for Federal assistance. This ruleset defines and refines acceptable documentation and report levels, state and regional contexts for National Register eligibility, sufficiency of due diligence in assessing project alternatives, most acceptable adverse effect mitigations, and so forth. "Neighborhood 106" can be a bit confusing for Agency Officials and applicants who deal cross-border with more than one SHPO.

Furthermore, since we know that, within the universe of Section 106 review players, not all are rational, or, for that matter, 'common knowledgeable', it seems realistic to presume that not all players will possess 'common knowledge' about the Section 106 review game, its formal and informal rules of play, its permitted strategies, and its allowable payoffs. Therefore, for there to be games that are amenable to Game Theory's maxims, Agency Officials and SHPOs must make sure that all players, even those who may prove to be irrational, are exposed to as much 'common knowledge' as can be before play begins. The easiest and best method for doing this is to ensure that all players are made aware of the formal rules codified at 36 CFR 800 plus any interpretations of those rules peculiar to an individual SHPO. Furthermore, SHPOs must themselves be prompt and forthcoming with any commonly-held information concerning the existence of known Cultural Resources and Historic Properties located within the Undertaking's mutually-defined APE.

'FOCAL POINTS'

"Now join your hands, and with your hands your hearts."
- William Shakespeare

Long years of agency, applicant, SHPO/THPO cooperation in Section 106 review spawn the reward of dramatically decreased risk and increased positive payoff. This state of continuous cooperation over time among the various participants in Section 106 review can even reach a point where consultative communication on a case-by-case basis may have been rendered almost un-necessary. To illustrate the point that close communication is not always essential to successful human interactions, there is the now-classic experiment in which Professor T. C. Schelling, of Cold War fame, informed certain of his students that they were to meet a stranger somewhere in New York City. Schelling had instructed that stranger to meet each student separately somewhere in the city but had given no directions as to the place or time of that meeting. No student would be allowed to communicate with the stranger to make appropriate arrangements.

Schelling then asked each student individually where he or she might have the best chance of finding this stranger and at what best time. The overwhelming majority responded, "Grand Central Terminal at noon".

Game Theorists refer to those places, times, and circumstances considered more or less 'common currency' by us all as 'Focal Points' or 'Schelling Points'. Focal points are so much a part of our daily experiences that most of us can identify them and use them to coordinate with others, even if a lack of complete communication precludes us from confirming with them. "Meet me at the same old place at the same old time," is not at all nonsensical among individuals with long experience of each other.

In Section 106 review, all participants know – because they have studied the rules of the game codified at 36 CFR 800.3 through .6 -- that the SHPO must respond to a review request within 30 days of receipt or be assumed to have concurred with the Agency Official's determinations and findings. Awareness of this 'Focal Point', therefore, precludes any real need on the part of a rational Agency Official or applicant to waste time asking the SHPO about it. Another 'Focal Point' involves the requirement codified at 36 CFR 800 that the Agency Official must seek consultation with the SHPO at each Step in the process. Therefore, there is no need for Agency Official requests for confirmation concerning whether or not she should seek the comments of the SHPO before she moves to the next Step.

These and a number of other similar types of 'Focal Points' result directly from the rulemaking codified at 36 CFR 800. Still other Focal Points evolve naturally from continuous common usage among the participants (see 'Neighborhood Monopoly'). They pertain to consistency in expected documentation levels, mutual agreement concerning the appropriate times and places for calling meetings and site visits, the mutually-accepted qualifications of consultants, the contexts that overarch various groupings of Cultural Resources than make them National Register eligible districts or not, and so forth. These and other similar Focal Points remove a great deal of the potential for confusion and confrontation in Section 106 review even if the level of communication among the participants concerning individual cases may have been diminished or temporarily cut off.

SECTION 106 AND GAME THEORY

INFLUENCES THAT PRE-DETERMINE THE COURSE OF THE GAME

"Some people were born to the shape they would occupy all their lives"
- *Conrad Williams*

Influences

According to Game Theorists, there are certain universal influences at work that pre-determine the course of any game played within a particular analogous range. These influences are:

1) the **relative values or 'utilities' of the final payoffs** that motivate each player either to retire from a losing game (low value payoffs) or to continue playing in expectation of eventual success (high value payoffs)
2) the **'attraction of distraction'**, or the tendency of a player to be distracted by the moves of other players to the point of losing sight of her own strategies and goals
3) the **rational (or irrational) manner** in which the players play the game
4) the **level of freedom** the players possess to communicate among themselves
5) the **cooperative or competitive personalities** of the players, and
6) the **ancillary risks** involving time, level of effort, and funds that are associated with playing any game

SECTION 106 AND GAME THEORY

Home Truths

Additionally, Game Theorists have distilled a set of 'home truths' at work that conspire to pre-determine a game's outcome. With respect to Section 106 review:

1) **If** and only **if** all its players have *accepted the existence of a common set of payoffs* that will reward each of them in some fashion, while punishing none severely, **then** a game will end cooperatively and successfully at whatever round is appropriate.

EXAMPLE: **if**, no Historic Properties have been identified during consultation, and **if** the Agency Official receives concurrence letters from the SHPO/THPO and other players, **then** she will happily resign from play with no challenges at the end of Step Two with a "No Historic Properties Affected," payoff.

EXAMPLE: After due consultation, an SHPO convinces an Agency Official to review a non-impactful alternative to her proposed Undertaking. This would end Step Three play by avoiding adverse effects to a Historic Property. **If** the Agency Official's assessment of the SHPO's suggested alternative has proved it both prudent and feasible, while meeting her project's original purpose and need, **then** she will willingly shift her preference to that avoidance alternative. Both Agency Official and SHPO will see the payoff as a 'win'.

2) **If** they expect to win in the long term, **then** all participants in the review game must *play fairly and strictly according to the rules, both formal and informal*.

EXAMPLE: **If** an irrational Agency Official fabricates evidence supporting a determination of National Register ineligibility and

if that fabrication is discovered by the SHPO while reviewing the Agency Official's Cultural Resources survey report, **then** that will indicate the sort of purposeful bad acting on the Agency Official's part that well might predispose the other players to retire, leaving the game unresolved. This wholesale abandonment would consign the Agency Official to the not so tender mercies of the ACHP.

In such instances, all participants lose.

3) **If** the Agency Official attempts to *foster an atmosphere of free interchange of information among participants*, **then** she will have taken a major step toward cooperative, mutually-beneficial completion of the process. This is true, even **if** the Agency Official must modify her Undertaking as originally proposed to avoid or minimize the potential for adverse effect.

EXAMPLE: **If** a Consulting Party who enters the game of Section 106 review is already *pre-disposed to be confrontational* with an Agency Official, **then** he *risks failure in the game*. **If** met with a confrontational strategy, **then** the Agency Official quite likely will respond with confrontation as well. **If** the Consulting Party does not counter with a more cooperative attitude, **then** the risk of meltdown increases exponentially.

4) Contrariwise, a Consulting Party who *acts cooperatively*, even **if** the proposed Undertaking threatens a Historic Property, will reassure the Agency Official that he is *willing to consult further* to seek common solutions that will

protect the resource as much as possible while fulfilling the Undertaking's mission.

Federal Undertakings, like all other kinds of projects, contain all sorts of risks project managers must run; risks that involve pressures of time, funding, and staffing; the amount of review and oversight; and so forth. **If** Consulting Parties *demonstrate their awareness of the ancillary risks* associated with carrying out the Undertaking under Section 106 review, **then** they will accumulate much good will and a cooperative attitude from the Agency Official responsible for implementing that Undertaking.

Win or lose, these influences guide and shape the course of Section 106 review game play, and, to a great extent, they determine its success or failure.

GRAPHICAL TOOLS

"The mechanic that would perfect his work must first sharpen his tools."
- *Confucius*

The Decision-Payoff Matrix

Game Theorists have conveniently arranged for players to have a set of graphical devices so they may visualize their assignment and re-assignment of goals, strategies, and relative payoff values as game play begins and continues. They refer to one of these devices as a 'Decision-Payoff Matrix'. Decision-Payoff Matrices have proven very helpful in focusing players' minds on the game's various evolutions and their own roles and responses during the course of the game.

EXAMPLE: Here is a gambit from a typical Section 106 review case graphically represented in a series of Decision-Payoff Matrices. To demonstrate the uses of a Decision-Payoff Matrix, I have modified an example taken from "Solution Manual Game Theory: An Introduction" (Steve Tadelis, January 31, 2013) to demonstrate my point.

This gambit is called, "Selecting an Undertaking's Preferred Alternative".

An Agency Official must make a choice between two alternatives that involve demolition of certain above-ground Historic Properties within the project's APE. Each alternative would meet the purpose and need of her Undertaking and each was determined equally prudent and feasible. The Agency Official had done sufficient due diligence to know that there were no other prudent or feasible alternatives that met the Undertaking's purpose and need, and the SHPO had concurred. Furthermore, each of the Agency Official's two alternative were assessed at the beginning of the design development phase as equal to the other in terms of basic project-related cost, time, and effort.

During a preliminary survey of Cultural Resources conducted during the Step Two round of Section 106 review, the Agency Official had discovered that Alternative 'A''s APE contained three National Register listed Historic Properties. Alternative 'B''s alternative, however, contained only one Historic Property. Therefore, she assigned Alternative 'A' -3 value points because of the proportionate additional time, effort, and money she must expend during Step Four necessitated by the requirement to mitigate the adverse effect of demolition upon the three Historic Properties. She assigned Alternative 'B' -1 value point because she believed it would cost her proportionately less time, effort, and money during Step Four to mitigate the demolition of that one Historic Property.

SECTION 106 AND GAME THEORY

At this point, with all other project-related conditions being equal, and mindful of the budgeting associated with the relative costs, the Agency Official formally opted for Alternative 'B' as her preferred alternative.

As the game progressed through Step Four, the Agency Official became even more certain she had made the correct choice. She therefore formally 'bid' Alternative 'B' as her preferred alternative to the SHPO and the other players.

However, her assessment of the relative costs of her project alternatives had not taken into consideration the fact that, up until she bid Alternative 'B', she had consulted with none of the other participants in Section 106 review concerning the relative significance of the Historic Properties proposed for demolition. Responding to her 'bid', the SHPO pointed out to her, with some curtness, that the three Historic Properties identified in Alternative 'A' were three houses that comprised a small, locally-significant Historic District eligible for the National Register only under Criterion 'C' for architecture. Contrariwise, the one Historic Property identified in Alternative 'B' was an individually eligible building of national significance whose eligibility was sustained by three of the four National Register Criteria (significant events, people, and architecture).

The SHPO estimated that appropriate mitigation of the adverse effect to the three Historic Properties located within Alternative 'A' would be three times less impactful than the mitigation of the adverse effect to the one Historic Property located within Alternative 'B'.

At this point, the ruleset of the game codified at 36 CFR 800 compelled the Agency Official to re-think her original assignment of value points in the selection of a preferred alternative. In the end, she was inclined to alter her original decision and opt for Alternative 'A' instead, especially as the SHPO and a number of the other players challenged her original selection because of the increased project-related difficulties in mitigating adverse effect associated with a Historic Property of that high level of significance. The SHPO's revelation about the relative 'value' of the Historic Properties located in her APE would have been quite likely to have altered the Agency Official's final 'bid'.

Game Theorists often express players' pre-game orderings, subsequent interactions, and the resulting modifications they agree to as a Decision Payoff Matrix. The Agency Official in the previous example was obviously unaware that Section 106 review game rules require continuous, complete, interdependent, and flexible consultation among the players from beginning to end of play to preclude the sort of uninformed initial 'bid' as the one she made. Game Theory presumes that, while an individual player such as an Agency Official may set and order her goals before play, she cannot actually play the game by herself, thereby always suiting her strategies to her own goals. As a rational player, she must be ready to modify her pre-game decisions during play based upon her interactions with other players. For purposes of clarification, here is a set of Decision Payoff Matrices that graphically express the course of game play in the foregoing example.

SECTION 106 AND GAME THEORY

TABLE 1 DECISION PAYOFF MATRIX / STEP FOUR / BEGINNING

	Alternative 'A'	Alternative 'B' (Preferred)
Agency Official	Three Historic Properties / -3 (money, time, and effort)	One Historic Property / -1 (money, time, and effort)
SHPO	Three Historic Properties / +1 (level of significance)	One Historic Property / +3 (level of significance)
	Alternative 'A' (Preferred)	Alternative 'B'

The Agency Official and the SHPO from our last example are the two players represented in the preceding Decision Payoff Matrix depicting the state of play after the Agency Official has submitted her effect finding to consultation review in Step Four based upon her National Register determination. Following Agency Official/SHPO consultation concerning the relative significance of the Historic Properties being adversely affected, the Agency Official determined to opt for Alternative "A", here graphically represented.

TABLE 2 DECISION PAYOFF MATRIX / STEP FOUR / END

Agency Official	Alternative 'A'
	Three Historic Properties / +1 (level of significance)
	Alternative 'A' (Preferred)

The Agency Officials originally perceived the least cost to her in Alternative 'B' based purely on the relative number of Historic Properties identified in the APE while the SHPO perceived the least cost in Alternative 'A' based purely upon the relative significance of the Historic Properties. Once the Agency Official understood the relative utilities of the Historic Properties, it is quite certain that further consultation between the two participants will strike a bargain of some sort that will be reflected in the mitigation stipulations represented in the conditions of the drafted agreement document.

A CHALLENGE TO GAME THEORY: PROFESSOR STANLEY K. RIDGLEY

"Without contraries there is no progression. Attraction and repulsion, reason and energy, love and hate, are necessary to human existence."
- *William Blake*

By way of preface, Professor Ridgley *does* acknowledge the usefulness of Game Theory as a practical tool for the estimation of the best goals and strategies *rational* game players can and should bring to the table. Nevertheless, Ridgley believes that Game Theory cannot be trusted to formulate optimal goals and strategies in complex or nuanced games. Two reasons preclude it. First, multi-player games impose too much in the way of 'background noise' that confuses players' ability to comprehend the actions of other players. Second, as most Game Theorists themselves acknowledge, not all game players are *rational*.

In the real world, bitter experience proves Ridgley to be correct within certain parameters. For example, a small percentage of Section 106 review's Formal Consulting Parties Meetings *will* be burdened with irrational, emotional, and unpredictable players whose goals and strategies are out of joint with rational behavior. Then too, complex Undertakings that bring together numbers of individuals and groups with differing needs, goals, and strategies tend to complicate any sort of reasonable assessment of 'best play' goals and strategies.

Furthermore, Ridgley points to the 'friction' all players may reasonably expect to encounter during the course of a game. This 'friction', so clearly described by one of the 19th. Century's foremost analyst of military conflict, Carl von Clausewitz, is composed of what

Clausewitz considers the inescapable factors of 'uncertainty' and 'chance' that resist forward motion.

According to Ridgley, this 'friction' composed of uncertainty and chance often hinders the attainment of the very high-value, low-risk payoffs of rational game play that Game Theory champions. A sudden, un-predicted thunderstorm may delay a site visit that would have solved a dispute over National Register eligibility. Uncertainty over a complete listing of the Cultural Resource components of an APE may cause an Agency Official unintentionally to submit less-than-adequate support documentation to the SHPO, resulting in a time-consuming 'do over'.

Because of the possibility of irrational game play, complications resulting from a nuanced Undertaking, and the specter of uncertainty and chance that hovers over all Section 106 review consultations, Dr. Ridgley's caveats concerning Game Theory's utility in conflict resolution turn out to be quite compelling, but not necessarily damning of the validity of Game Theory.

Admittedly, irrational, emotional, and unpredictable participants and chance events have plagued certain Section 106 review cases in the past and will continue to do so in the future. These irrational players have increased the level of uncertainty in the process by using dishonorable strategies in an attempt to gain their un-realistic goals. However, the participants in the vast majority of Section 106 reviews with whom I have been involved over the past thirty plus years have not been irrational players. Instead, they have brought with them reasonable goals and appropriate strategies for attaining them. Furthermore, some participants in a Section 106 review game concerning a complicated Undertaking *may well have* brought goals to the table that differed from those of other players. However, they seldom saw themselves as true adversaries, either of each other or of the process. They showed themselves to be quite willing and able to consult together to find common ground. They were committed to playing by the rules.

For them and their like, the lessons of Game Theory most certainly would still apply.

As for Clausewitz's 'chance', it is admittedly a factor to be reckoned with, but, happily, not a very significant one in Section 106 review. As Dr. Stevens points out, the inherent limitations built into the rules of most games preclude randomness among the players' strategies, compelling them to employ, 'pure strategies' as Game Theorists would define them. These strategies derive directly from the rules of the game that instruct players as to what they are allowed to do in nearly every situation. The Section 106 rulebook -- the 36 CFR 800 Regulation -- does an excellent job of this. It leaves little room for uncertainty or chance.

In real life, that dreaded Boing 787 which is the modern bugbear example of Clausewitz's 'friction' never really does fall from the sky to crash land onto the Section 106 consultation table just as the participants have reached consensus on the issues that brought them together.

ACKNOWLEDGED LIMITS

"Limits, like fear, is often an illusion."
- Michael Jordan

Analogous Predictive Analysis suggests that any two games, whether simple or complex, that exhibit the same identifiable and mathematically quantifiable ranges of traits by category, are likely subjects for Game Theory algorithmic evaluation and analysis. Positive strategies and goals that win in 'low stakes' game will also win when used in their 'high stakes' counterparts. Even so, Game Theory makes us aware that the very types of games whose goals, strategies, and outcomes Game Theory modeling can most accurately identify and quantify are simple, two-player board games like Checkers or NIM. For this reason, where feasible, one should attempt to collect individual participants in a Section 106 review game into 'sets' of players with common goals and strategies, just as I did during the earlier discussion of Utility Theory and 'dominant' goals.

As Professor Benjamin points out correctly, "The more players, the more complex the strategy". Professor Stevens expands upon this notion by stating, "Adding complexity to a game can quickly increase the number of possible strategies". We already know that Section 106 review begins with a minimum of five players, making it somewhat less predictable from the outset than if it were strictly a two-player game. The more players there are who participate and the more nuanced the game becomes; the more difficult it is to identify its most positive goals and strategies and to pre-solve its outcome with infallible mathematical accuracy.

These facts in no way signify that Game Theory modeling and the lessons learned from it are valueless to those who 'coach' more nuanced games such as Section 106 review. Few, if any, of those involved in that review process are mathematicians anyway. Therefore, we may, like Professor Neilson, and with few apologies, skip over most of the intricate mathematical modeling that accompanies advanced Game Theory and concentrate instead upon what we know from years of experience to be the dynamics of the process, using what Game Theory lessons we can as best we can.

INTERLUDE: "THE PRISONER'S DILEMMA"

"The iterated "prisoner's dilemma" has become such a popular subject for psychological studies that political scientist Robert Axelrod dubbed it the 'E. Coli of social psychology...'"
- William Poundstone

Before going any further, I wish to pause to introduce readers to a canonical little exercise to which Game Theorists often refer. It will appear later in the book, so we may as well discuss it now. This iconic game serves as a commonly used test bench for Game Theorists to prove, or dis-prove, their derived mathematical models, and is, therefore, well worth becoming familiar with. It goes by the name of 'The Prisoner's Dilemma'.

In this game, the local detective squad suspects two men of having committing the same burglary together because beat patrolmen apprehended them in each other's company near the scene of the burglary right after it was reported; each suspect with half a set of burglar tools in his possession. The police formally arrest them both on suspicion of a felony and place them in separate interrogation rooms. The police know from years of experience that, by preventing their suspects from overhearing each other during interrogation, their interrogators are more likely to make one or the other confess to the crime. Game Theorists refer to this confession as a 'defection' because the one who confesses is defecting from his loyalty to his partner in crime.

Author's Note - Please remember that Merrill Flood and Melvin Dresher, working at the RAND Corporation in 1950, created the scenario that eventually

SECTION 106 AND GAME THEORY

became The 'Prisoner's Dilemma' 16 years before Miranda v. Arizona (1966).

During interrogation, each prisoner has one of only two choices. He may either confess or stand mute. Circumstances preclude his being able to claim innocence. The police interrogators have explained the consequences of each available choice to each prisoner separately. One prisoner may confess, turn states evidence against his partner in crime, and serve no prison time at all while his partner receives a twenty-year sentence. Both may confess simultaneously, independent of each other, and each will then receive a five-year sentence. Both may stand mute independent of each other and each will receive only a one-year sentence for being apprehended in possession of burglar tools.

Here is the dilemma each prisoner faces. He does not know what his partner in crime will do; confess (defect) or stand mute (remain loyal). The only thing he does know is, **if** he confesses immediately and his partner stands mute, **then** he goes free while his partner spends twenty years in prison. **If** he stands mute and his partner confesses immediately, **then** the tables are turned. **If** both confess simultaneously, **then** each receives a five-year sentence. **If** both stand mute, **then** each receives only a one-year sentence.

Obviously, either prisoner may decide to 'defect' against the other by confessing immediately. Some Game Theorists contend that this is the best course of action. They maintain that, because betraying his partner in crime offers a greater reward than cooperating with him, all purely rational self-interested prisoners would betray the other. So the only rational outcome for the two self-interested prisoners is for them to betray each other. **If** either does confess while his partner in crime stands mute, **then** he will go free. At this point, and **if** this *is* the best course of action, **then** the only important question remains, 'which one will confess first?' **If**, however, each prisoner decides independently to 'cooperate' with the other prisoner by trusting his partner to do just the same thing as he does himself, **then** the worst each can receive by way of punishment is a five-year sentence (both confess simultaneously) and at best, merely a one-year sentence (both stand mute simultaneously).

Furthermore, **if** both had agreed, "cross your heart, and hope to die", before the burglary to 'cooperate', by standing mute **if** caught, **then** so much the better because neither one would need to wonder what his partner was going to do. There are a number of reasons why the two erstwhile burglars would agree beforehand to stand mute if arrested. Both may be brothers whose mutual self-interest is tied to family. Furthermore, each may realize that "ratting" on his partner would sully his reputation in the criminal community in which he operates. Still furthermore, when informed of the light sentence each would receive if he stands mute, either prisoner would see keeping to the agreement made before the burglary as in his self-interest.

The takeaway from a review of 'The Prisoner's Dilemma' scenario seems to be that competition ultimately costs more than cooperation. Its equally-important corollary is, "to ensure best payoffs, form cooperative alliances before the opening round of a game or as soon thereafter as possible".

We will return several times in the book to this neat benchmark game and discuss Game Theory's study of it.

PART THREE: GAME THEORY AND SECTION 106 REVIEW

TRUSTING GAME THEORY'S USEFULNESS IN SECTION 106 REVIEW

"Everybody is playing games. There are games now for pretty much every age, every demographic."
- *Jesse Schell*

More than thirty years of relevant experience with the Section 106 review process teaches that all rational participants in that process come to the consultation table with some sorts of pre-conceived notions of what they wish to accomplish as individual players and some ideas about how they wish to attain their goals. If asked, they will readily and unabashedly admit at the beginning of a Section 106 review game that they are sitting at the consultation table for no other reason than to attain what they consider their self-interest-defined utility (their own highest relative value or lowest relative risk). As play continues, participants observe the strategies of their fellow players and the goals those strategies seek to attain. At appropriate times during the game, participants may modify their own goals and strategies to suit the current situation.

The laws of rationality require that those who participate in Section 106 review must have some sort of assurance that, at the end of the day, they have chosen the *right* utility and the *right* strategy for attaining it. The lessons learned from Utility Theory combined with those learned from Prospect Theory offer such assurances.

Over the past half-century, Game Theory has gained quite an impressive reputation for identifying these best player goals and strategies in a wide variety of 'real world' situations. The proof of the validity of analogous predictive analysis lies within that record of accomplishment (The MAD strategy that stalemated the Cold War is only the most well-known example.).

Given this track record, rational participants in Section 106 review should be more than willing to trust the notion that Game Theory's methods can be used effectively to evaluate an initial range of goals and strategies offered by the rules written into 36 CFR 800 and modify them as needs be in response to the actions of other participants.

Based upon the outcome of this initial Utility Theory evaluation and enlightened by the tenets of Prospect Theory, rational participants will come to understand the need to re-define their own highest utilities and accompanying strategies during each Section 106 review game as it moves through a series of interactions with other participants.

Furthermore, once a participant feels his re-defined strategies will attain his highest value payoffs, he should seek to identify those goals shared with other players through interdependent consultation. Then, he may well suggest that other like-minded participants join forces to attain common goals.

IS IT REALLY A GAME?

"To be able to ask a question clearly is two-thirds of the way to getting it answered."
- *John Ruskin*

After having read the preceding pages, rational participants in Section 106 review should see a decided advantage in using the rules of Game Theory to help them identify both their individual and their common utilities as well as the best strategies for attaining them.

If they were indeed persuaded to view Section 106 review as a 'game' subject to analogous predictive analysis, **then** they could be expected to speculate about just what practical advantages Game Theory could offer them.

Therefore, let's begin to answer this key question by using Dr. Ridgley and Dr. Stevens' definition of a game. Ridgley states that a game is...

1.) a series of <u>interactions</u> among <u>rational players</u> (Dr. Stevens refers to them as 'decision makers') who are

2.) striving to make the best of a <u>set of allowable moves</u>, referred to as <u>'strategies'</u> (Dr. Stevens refers to them as 'decisions for each possible situation in which a player may find himself or herself'), because these players are

3.) motivated by the <u>desire to attain certain goals</u> referred to as 'payoffs' or 'utility functions' (Dr. Stevens refers to these as 'the reward or loss a player experiences when all the players follow their respective strategies'), and

4.) their goals and strategies for attaining these 'payoffs' are <u>interdependent</u> with the goals and strategies of the other players

I propose that Section 106 review easily meets Ridgley and Stevens' definitions because it is:

1.) a series of ordered (as defined at 36 CFR 800.3 through .6) **interactions** among rational players:

- a Federal Agency Official (or an applicant for Federal funds, licenses, permits, or approvals)
- a State Historic Preservation Officer (SHPO)
- a Tribal Historic Preservation Officer (THPO)
- Tribal Representatives or Native Hawaiian Organization Representatives
- Representatives of local government
- Affected property owners, and
- Individuals or groups with standing because of economic interest or historic preservation interest in the Federal Undertaking under review.

2.) These players are striving to make the best of **a set of allowable moves (strategies)** codified at 36 CFR 800,

3.) because they are motivated by the desire **to attain certain goals** that they bring to the consultation table,

4.) and these goals are **interdependent** with those of the other players.

When the Section 106 review game begins, the Agency Official sees her highest utility as a speedy, low risk, and compliant end to the process. The SHPO/THPO/Tribe's highest utility is the identification, evaluation, and protection of threatened Historic Properties. Other participants begin with their own self-interested highest utilities that they wish to attain as the game progresses. During game play, the self-defined utility of each player may shift a bit, based upon the actions of the other players and each player's shifting take on those actions.

So long as these players continue to use rational strategies allowable under the rules of the game codified at 36 CFR 800 interdependently to attain certain desirable goals pertaining to National Register of Historic Places (NTHP) eligibility, assessment of project effect upon Historic Properties, and the resolution of project-related adverse effect, they will enhance their chances of completing the game successfully. To do this, the participants in a Section 106 review game must somehow continue to reason together through **interactive and interdependent consultation**, even when discussions over certain Federal Undertakings offer them less-than-complete information about NRHP eligibility, project-related effects, or the best ways to resolve adverse effect.

The Common Goal

Furthermore, whether the participants who play the game of Section 106 review realize it or not, the rules codified at 36 CFR 800 are drawing them all toward one common goal. If successfully played, the interdependence that results from the consultation required by 36 CFR 800 will guarantee they attain that common goal, which is **the successful completion of the process** with the least risk and the most value *for all*. This search for a common utility through consultative interdependent interaction that runs through the entire Section 106 review and is a requirement of 36 CFR 800 confirms it as a 'game' for purposes of this book.

'ANALOGOUS PREDICTIVE ANALYSIS' MODELING

"It has truly been said that in the life of every forest fire, a mere cup of water, prudently poured over it at the proper time, would have snuffed it out."
- *Unknown Source*

Since the 1960s, disciples of Game Theory have used analogous predictive analysis algorithms to search for that mathematical 'cup of water' that will snuff out the fire of conflict in high stakes games as well as in low stakes games. Admittedly, almost all Section 106 review cases exist in a realm where the payoffs are not nearly so weighty as in the 'high-stakes' sort, and the negative consequences of competition and conflict, though quite real, are nowhere near as devastating. Still, William L. Shirer was right when he wrote more than fifty years ago, "chaos may sometimes have gentle beginnings."

Those who have taken a leading role in games of Section 106 review struggle to bring order out of the chaos that is often synonymous with Federal environmental assessment. Therefore, they have good reason willingly to consider some of the lessons Game Theorists can teach about conflict prevention and resolution in high-stakes games. This is so because these lessons derive from the trustworthy mathematical analysis of analogous low-stakes games. By paying attention to these lessons, they can better assist those game players with whom they interact to see the differences between 'good' and 'bad' goals. They can help them rank 'good' goals in comparative order of value. They can encourage participants to work toward a flexible strategy in game play that allows for easy adjustment in the rank order of goals as the game moves forward. They can share knowledge about honorable strategies participants may use with confidence to attain their goals. They can encourage participants to recognize and reject dishonorable strategies. They can encourage participants to form binding agreements that resolve project-related adverse effects to Historic Properties.

Today, Game Theory with its analogous predictive analysis is shedding much-needed light on all sorts of complex and nuanced "high-stakes" interactions where conflict is likely. It offers the welcome possibility of resolving those interactions in ways that may actually keep them resolved.

CATEGORIES BY OBJECT OF THE GAME

"I think the reason that I like so many different games is because I like the way my brain works when I'm playing games. It's more fun."
- John Romero

For purposes of this book I have continued to refer to the consultative review process mandated by Section 106 of the NHPA as a 'game', complete with rules, players, rounds of play, strategies, tactics, goals, and payoffs (both positive and negative) at its end. Furthermore, **if** Section 106 review *is* a game, **then** it is susceptible to analogous predictive analysis. However, merely referring to Section 106 review as a game is insufficient to actually making it into one. Remember Abraham Lincoln's sardonic question, "How many legs does a dog have if you call the tail a leg? Four! Calling a tail a leg doesn't make it a leg."

At this point, a discerning reader may well say, "**If** Section 106 review really *is* a game, so what!"

"If it is to be of any use to us, **then** it must be a member of a specific game *category* and be amenable to analogous predictive analysis."

Here, Professor Arthur Benjamin offers some helpful insight. He proposes that almost all 'games of sequence', where move follows move in a pre-determined order, fall into one of three categories, defined by each category's game object.

1) The winning object of Dr. Benjamin's first game category is to **amass the most stuff**, as in Monopoly where winning depends upon accumulating the greatest amount of valuable property from which rental income may be derived. As we have just seen, Section 106 review does not automatically place increased emphasis or value upon projects whose Areas of Potential Effects (APE) contain a greater number of Historic Properties against those that contain fewer ones. One Historic Property affected by a Federal Undertaking requires the same order of effect assessment under Step Three of Section 106 review as 100 such. Furthermore, if only one contributing Historic Property within a Historic District is directly affected by a Federal Undertaking, this is the same as if an individually-eligible Historic Property were being affected because the effect will reverberate throughout the historic district.

    Therefore, Section 106 review is clearly not a Category One game.

2) The winning object of Dr. Benjamin's second game category is to **create some sort of structure or ordered pattern**, as in Tic-Tac-Toe, where winning involves connecting an unbroken series of 'Xs' or 'O's. While Section 106 review has a defined structure of sequence from one Step to the next, achieving the end product of an executed Memorandum of Agreement has no value in and of itself if no Historic Properties had been identified within the Undertaking's

SECTION 106 AND GAME THEORY

APE, or the Undertaking was found not to adversely affect any Historic Properties discovered.

Section 106 review is clearly not of the 'follow-the-dots' variety and therefore is not a Category Two game. This fact is especially welcome to those of us who are involved with Section 106 review because 'best play' from both players of a game such as Tic-tac-toe can do no better than a draw.

3) The winning object of Dr. Benjamin's third game category is to **be the last player to move**, as in Poker, Checkers, Chess, or the taking game NIM. This category is most akin to Section 106 review, in that, while the Agency Official always has the opening move in each round of play, she does not always have the closing, or 'winning' move. Action and re-action follow along in sequence as the game proceeds through the required number of Section 106 review Steps until consensus has been achieved between the Agency Official or applicant and the SHPO/THPO or ACHP with respect to National Register eligibility, project effect, and resolution of adverse effect. The peculiar circumstances of each individual case dictate who has the last move, and therefore who 'wins' the game.

Therefore, Section 106 review is truly a 'game', complete with Professor Benjamin's "Category Three" object.

SECTION 106 AND GAME THEORY

A GAME OF SEQUENCE

"Never rush in haste for anything. Keep calm, stay focused, and the sequence of events will take care of itself."
- Anil Kr Sinha

Students of Game Theory agree that, at base, all 'games of sequence' naturally divide into ordered successions of separate and distinct rounds of play:

- **Opening Gambit** (establishing qualifications to play, taking possession of one's assigned portion of the game board, receiving one's initial set of tokens or cards, placing forced antes, if required, into the 'pot', making opening moves to 'test the water')

- **Midgame** (discovery of opponent strategies, analysis and re-ordering of one's own strategies, maneuver, and counter-maneuver)

- **Resolution or Endgame** (final showdown) that awards payoffs to the winner

Using this succession of game play as our guide, we can declare that Section 106 review is a true game of sequence. Its opening gambit is 'Step One / Initiation of the Section 106 review Process'. Its midgame plus its endgame can either be 'Step Two / Identification of Historic Properties', or 'Step Three / Assessment of Adverse Effects', or 'Step Four / Resolution of Adverse Effects', depending upon the outcome of the previous Step's end of play and where the review of a particular Undertaking is lodged at any point in time.

It has been my experience that approximately 85% of all Section 106 review games divide play between two of these sequential rounds (Step One – Initiate the Process and Step Two – Evaluate Historic

Properties) with an endgame consensus determination that "no Historic Properties are affected".

However**,** **if** consensus among the players determines that a Historic Property is located within the Undertaking's APE, **then** a further 13% add a round (Step Three — Assess Project Effect) that ends with a consensus endgame finding that "no Historic Properties are adversely affected".

If consensus among the players finds project-related adverse effect, **then** the remaining two percent add a further round (Step Four — Resolve Adverse Effects) with a consensus endgame resolution of that adverse effect.

Because of this ordered sequence of Steps, or rounds, the Section 106 review process is sufficiently like other 'games of sequence' to be open to a fair analysis, assessment, and comparison with other games using the methods of modern Game Theory.

CATALOGUED BY TYPE

"Cataloguing is an ancient profession; there are examples of such "ordainers of the universe" (as they were called by the Sumerians) among the oldest vestiges of libraries."
- Alberto Manguel

Cataloguing Section 106 Review

Over the last five decades, modern Game Theorists have put forward a set of delimiters that catalog analogous ranges of games by typology. Using these delimiters, we can reasonably state that Section 106 review is a game that is:

1) meant to be **cooperative** – rather than competitive – because its rules encourage all participants to:
    a. consult freely and flexibly among each other throughout the game
    b. share information without restriction or reservation
    c. form cooperative alliances, and
    d. craft binding end-game commitments, if need be, in the form of agreement documents that require players to adhere to the promises they have made in previous rounds

Dr. Stevens points out that only cooperative games such as Section 106 review make it possible for players to consult freely, share information, form alliances, and craft binding end-game agreements. In non-cooperative gamers, such player interaction is made impossible by the rules of the game. In fact, any type of free communication such as signaling, information sharing about the values of their hands, alliance forming, and endgame agreements to split the 'pot' among the players during competitive game play is considered cheating.

The clear intent of the ACHP Framers who codified the rules governing Section 106 review at 36 CFR 800 was that this process would be a cooperative endeavor, based upon continuous, interdependent consultation and consensus building among its primary players. Sadly, however, the benign intentions of the Framers and their ordered procedures have not always prevented conflict among certain players during real world game play. However, the principles of Game Theory may well provide the techniques necessary to transform conflict into cooperation.

2) ***not* a 'zero-sum' game** because, in such games, a player benefits only at the equal and opposite expense of another player. This is not true in Section 106 review, although some players have heatedly argued that it is.

3) **a 'sequential' game** allowing players who enter in later rounds of play to have received some beneficial knowledge about the actions of earlier players.

Morton Davis maintains that this need not be perfect knowledge about every action of earlier players -- it might actually be very little knowledge -- but there is always some advantageous knowledge available to latecomers.

4) **a game of 'imperfect information'** because all players do not necessarily know all the moves previously made by all other players or the relative values of their 'hands'.

Game Theorists refer to simple board games like Checkers as games of 'perfect information'. By this, they mean that, as play develops, both participants can see the entire game board at the same time. Nothing is hidden from them on the Checkerboard. This affords both players perfect information at every point during game play to help determine which strategies might best facilitate reaching their winning goal.

The original assemblage of Section 106 review rule-makers (staffers at the ACHP that I have referred to as 'Framers') may well have aspired to creating just such a game of perfect information as they drafted the first iteration of 36 CFR 800. Ideally, all Section 106 review participants would:

      a. move through the sequential Steps at the same pace

b. have simultaneous access to the same project narratives and Cultural Resources survey reports
c. attend project-related site visits at the same time
d. meet together formally at the same time to discuss the Undertaking under review, and
e. review and comment simultaneously upon Federal agency determinations and findings

However, like most 'games of chance', Section 106 review as practiced in the real world became 'chancy' simply because circumstances of time, place, and expense always seemed to conspire to prevent its players from seeing all other players 'hands' all at the same time. Therefore, its participants will always possess imperfect information and, because of this fact, they have become far less certain that a particular strategy will always attain their goal and win a positive payoff. Game Theorists refer to a process like Section 106 review as a game of 'imperfect information'.

5) a game of **random strategies** played by intelligent participants. In that way, Section 106 review is similar to Poker, Bridge, or Backgammon. It has a fixed sequence of play but a set of strategies and goals that is random because its players' goals and strategies are all subject to change as play progresses.

6) *not* a **'combinational game'** such as Monopoly that proceeds through a considerable number of rounds. There are only **a finite number of rounds** (a maximum of four Steps) allowed players by the rules of Section 106 review set down at 36 CFR 800 and the resulting games, therefore, are most always of relatively short duration.

7) completed within a **finite number of moves and counter-moves** (a maximum of nine moves); although it may seem otherwise to the participants in a protracted Section 106 review.
8) Composed of a **finite number of players**, (a minimum number of five players and a maximum number of eleven players). Because of this fact, games like Section 106 review are referred to by Game Theorists as 'n-person games'

To sum up, according to these catalogued Game Theory delimiters, Section 106 review is a **cooperative, non-zero-sum, random, sequential, non-combination, n-person Category Three game of imperfect information with a finite number of rounds, moves, and players**.

The Section 106 Review Game: The Rounds And The Moves Within Rounds List In Detail

As stated, there are only a finite number of rounds (a maximum of four Steps) and a finite number of moves (a maximum of nine moves and counter-moves) allowed players by the rules of Section 106 review set down at 36 CFR 800. These are:

1) Initiate the Section 106 Process
    a) Establish Undertaking
    b) Identify Appropriate SHPO/THPO
    c) Plan to Involve the Public
    d) Identify Other Consulting Parties
2) Identify Historic Properties
    a) Determine Scope of Efforts

b) Identify Historic Properties
   c) Evaluate Historic Significance
3) Assess Adverse Effect
   a) Apply Criteria of Adverse Effect
4) Resolve Adverse Effect
   a) Continue Consultation

The Section 106 Review Game: The Players List In Detail

Section 106 review has its unique set of players duly listed at 36 CFR 800.2. The mandatory number of players in each game may be as few as five or as many as eleven. The final number of players depends upon the size and scale of the Federal Undertaking under review, the geographic size of its Area of Potential Effects (APE), the number and type of Historic Properties affected, the nature of project-related effect, and the level of difficulty in resolving any project-associated adverse effect.

The Section 106 review game's set of players is a collection of defined participant placeholders, all of whom have standing (an undeniable stake in the outcome of the process). They include:

1) the **Federal Agency Official** tasked with the responsibility of implementing a Federal Undertaking subject to Section 106 review
2) the **Advisory Council on Historic Preservation** (ACHP) tasked with the responsibility of monitoring whether the rules of the Section 106 review game are followed
3) the **State Historic Preservation Officer** (SHPO) tasked with the responsibility of assisting, advising, and

cooperating with the Agency Official as she identifies, evaluates, and takes into account the Cultural Resources and Historic Properties located within the Undertaking's APE

4) the **Tribal Historic Preservation Officer** (THPO) tasked with the responsibility of identifying, evaluating, and protecting the significant cultural and religious resources located on his tribal lands

5) the authorized **representatives of Indian tribes and Native Hawaiian Organizations** tasked with the responsibility of identifying, evaluating, and protecting significant cultural and religious resources located off tribal lands

6) the authorized **representatives of local governments** tasked with the responsibility of representing the 'best land use interests' of their jurisdictions

7) the **applicants** for Federal funds, licenses, permits, and approvals of one sort or another, tasked with the responsibility of obtaining that assistance promptly and with the least possible risk

8) the affected public and private **property owners**, tasked with the responsibility of obtaining the best and fullest use of their properties

9) the **other parties** with a specific economic interest in a Federal Undertaking that affords them standing

10) the **other parties** with a specific historic preservation interest in a Federal Undertaking that affords them standing

11) the **Public**

RULES, PLAYERS, SUCCESSIVE ROUNDS, BIDDING SEQUENCE, AND ANALYSIS OF PLAY

"A lot of people think international relations is like a game of chess. But it's not a game of chess, where people sit quietly, thinking out their strategy, taking their time between moves. It's more like a game of billiards, with a bunch of balls clustered together."
- *Madeleine Albright*

Like all games worth playing, Section 106 review must be played according to a clear set of rules all rational and intelligent players agree to abide by to stay in the game. As we already know, the ruleset of Section 106 review is contained within the language of 36 CFR 800.3 through .6. Additional 'special' rules having to do with specific players with sufficient standing to play may be found at 36 CFR 800.2 and other, subsidiary, rules are spread throughout other parts of the Regulation. A list of penalties for breaking the rules is codified at 36 CFR 800.7.

What follows is a rather truncated discussion of game play and an analysis of it. Highlighted action verbs either indicate formal bidding or player goal or strategy assessments made prior to bidding.

Play By Play

Opening Gambit / Initiation of the Section 106 Process / 36 CFR 800.3

SECTION 106 AND GAME THEORY

The Agency Official (opening or first player) **reviews** her proposed Federal project, program, or activity (her 'hand') and determines whether it is an Undertaking subject to Section 106 review (a 'biddable' hand). In making this determination, she must **use** the definition contained within the 36 CFR 800 Regulation. Here it is again for your convenience. "An Undertaking is a project, activity, or program funded in whole or in part under the direct or indirect jurisdiction of a Federal agency, including those carried out by or on behalf of a Federal agency; those carried out with Federal financial assistance; those requiring a Federal permit, license or approval; and those subject to State or local Regulation administered pursuant to a delegation or approval by a Federal agency". Then she **adds** the condition also contained within 36 CFR 800 that makes it subject to Section 106 review. Here is the condition. "...that *might* cause effect to a Historic Property eligible for listing in or listed in the National Register of Historic Places."

She evaluates her project using the definition of 'Undertaking', then applies the '**if-then**' condition of potential effect to establish whether it is subject to Section 106 review. **If** she determines her Undertaking is *not* subject to Section 106 review (while almost all Federal activities are Undertakings, a quite large percentage are not subject to Section 106 review because they have no potential to cause effects to Historic Properties), **then** she **resigns** from the game and there is no further play. Under game rules, other players may challenge her decision to resign from the game, and **if** they do so, **then** she must **show** valid reasons for making her decision to resign.

If she determines that her Undertaking *is* subject to Section 106 review, **then** she **opens play** by **identifying** the appropriate **State Historic Preservation Officer** (SHPO) (second player) and **begins consultation**. **If** the Undertaking is proposed on Tribal lands, **then** she also **identifies** the appropriate **Tribal Historic Preservation Officer** (THPO) (third (*possible*) player) and **begins consultation**.

Once she has identified and begun consultation with these players, serious game play begins. The Agency Official **'bids'** her hand by consulting with these players "in a manner appropriate to the agency planning process for the Undertaking and to the nature of the Undertaking and its effects on Historic Properties". In doing so, she refers to various guidance protocols contained within 36 CFR 800 as well as those provided by the Office of the Keeper of the National Register of Historic Places. She may also consult with the other players to make initial and tentative pre-consultation determinations of National Register of Historic Places eligibility concerning Cultural Resources located within her project's impact area (APE) and to make initial and tentative pre-consultation findings of her project's potential effects upon any National Register properties identified. She shares those tentative determinations and findings with the other players.

The SHPO/THPO has 30 days from the time of receipt of the Agency Official's formal **request for review** of her determinations and findings (**her 'bids'**) to **review** them. During that time, he may **withhold comment ('pass')**, **agree ('call')**, or **request additional information ('raise')** necessary to inform his final comment. **If** the SHPO and/or the THPO **fail to respond ('pass')** within 30 days of receipt of proper documentation, **then** the Agency Official may either **proceed** to the next step in the game based upon her finding or determination or **consult** with the **Advisory Council on Historic Preservation** (ACHP) (fourth (*possible*) player) in lieu of the other players. **If** the SHPO or the THPO decide to

SECTION 106 AND GAME THEORY

re-enter the Section 106 review game at a later round, **then** the Agency Official shall **continue** the consultation but **without being required to reconsider previous findings or determinations**.

Simultaneously, in consultation with the SHPO and/or the THPO, the Agency Official will plan to involve **the public** (fifth player) in the Section 106 process. Based upon her own agency's public information protocols, the Agency Official identifies the appropriate points for seeking public input and for notifying the public of proposed actions. She also **invites** appropriate **representatives of local government** (sixth player), **applicants for federal assistance** (funding, permits, licenses, or approvals) (seventh (*possible*) player), **affected property owners** (eighth (*possible*) player) and other individuals **if** they have a demonstrated interest in the Undertaking because of their **legal or economic relation to the Undertaking** (ninth (*possible*) player) or affected properties, or their **concern with the Undertaking's effects on Historic Properties** (tenth (*possible*) player). **If** the Undertaking is proposed off tribal lands, **then** she makes a good faith effort to **identify and invite** the appropriate **tribe or tribes or Native Hawaiian Organization** (eleventh (*possible*) player) that have demonstrated cultural or religious interest in the area. Furthermore, with the help of the SHPO, THPO, and tribal representatives, she **considers** all written requests of **individuals and organizations to participate as Consulting Parties** (*possible additional players*).

SECTION 106 AND GAME THEORY

Analysis

During the opening round of play, the various players become acquainted with each other and with the specific Undertaking under review. At this point in the game, a spirit of cooperation exists among all rational players as they review and comment upon the Agency Official's initial, pre-consultation determinations and findings, if any exist. There is hardly ever any controversy concerning the Agency Official's choice of the appropriate SHPO, or THPO (if the project is proposed on tribal land), because those choices are elementary and obvious. There may be some difference of opinion as to the identity and number of certain other Consulting Parties and the exact scope and scale of public involvement. However, consultation among the players usually ends in cooperation and consensus on these matters. Participants share a common goal defined as the timely and compliant completion of the process.

Next Round Play By Play

Midgame (Discovery, Analysis, And Maneuver) / Identification and Evaluation of Historic Properties / 36 CFR 800.4)

During this second round of the Section 106 review game, the various players **interact** through interdependent consultation ('bid' and 'counter bid') in an attempt to find consensus while the Agency Official **formulates** determinations of National Register of Historic Places eligibility/ineligibility concerning any Cultural Resources discovered within the Federal Undertaking's Area of Potential Effects (APE). The Agency Official **continues to consult** with the SHPO, a THPO (if, and only if, the Undertaking is proposed on tribal lands), and appropriate Tribal Representatives (if the proposed Undertaking is off

SECTION 106 AND GAME THEORY

Tribal lands), and other Consulting Parties. This consultation should eventually **reach consensus** concerning an appropriate scope of identification effort that the Agency Official shall make. This consensus **takes into account** the nature of the Undertaking, its size and scope, and the likelihood of encountering Historic Properties. The Agency Official then formally **determines ('bids')** what she considers to be an appropriate scope of effort for doing all this in consultation with the SHPO/THPO.

The next order of business for the Agency Official after consensus has been reached concerning scope of work is **finding consensus** on the Undertaking's Area of Potential Effects (APE). The APE is "the geographic area or areas within which an Undertaking may cause (directly or indirectly) alterations in the character or use of Historic Properties, if any such Historic Properties exist". The APE "is influenced by the scale and nature of an Undertaking and may be different for different kinds of effects caused by the Undertaking". The Agency Official **consults** with other players to review existing information on Historic Properties within the APE, including any data concerning possible Historic Properties not yet identified.

Based upon the information gathered, and **in consultation with** the SHPO/THPO and any Indian tribe or Native Hawaiian organization that might attach religious and cultural significance to properties within the APE, the Agency Official **takes the steps necessary** to identify Cultural Resources within the APE. She makes a reasonable and good faith effort to **carry out** appropriate identification efforts, which may include "background research, consultation, oral history interviews, sample field investigation, and field survey". She also **takes into account** "past planning, research and studies, the magnitude and nature of the Undertaking and the degree of

SECTION 106 AND GAME THEORY

Federal involvement, the nature and extent of potential effects on Historic Properties, and the likely nature and location of Historic Properties within the Area of Potential Effects".

In consultation with the SHPO/THPO and any Indian tribe or Native Hawaiian organization that attaches religious and cultural significance to identified Cultural Resources, the Agency Official **applies** the National Register criteria (36 CFR 63) to any Cultural Resources identified within the APE. **If** the Agency Official **determines** any of the National Register criteria are met after evaluating a Cultural Resource, and the SHPO/THPO **agrees, then** she **formally bids that determination** and the property shall be considered a Historic Property eligible for listing in the National Register for Section 106 purposes. **If** the Agency Official **determines** the criteria are not met and the SHPO/THPO **agrees, she bids that formal determination** and the Cultural Resource shall be considered not National Register eligible. **If** the Agency Official and the SHPO/THPO **do not agree**, or **if** the ACHP **requests, then** the Agency Official shall **obtain** a determination of National Register eligibility from the Office of the Keeper of the National Register of Historic Places pursuant to 36 CFR 63. **If** an Indian tribe or Native Hawaiian organization that attaches religious and cultural significance to a property off tribal lands **does not agree, then** it may **ask** the ACHP to **request** the Agency Official **obtain** a formal determination of eligibility from the Keeper.

If the Agency Official **determines** either 1) that there are no Historic Properties present or 2) that there are Historic Properties present but the Undertaking will have no effect upon them, **then** the Agency Official **provides support documentation** of this determination to the SHPO/THPO. The Agency Official **notifies** all current players, including Indian tribes and Native Hawaiian organizations, and **makes the documentation available** for public inspection before approving the Undertaking.

Endgame

If the SHPO/THPO or the ACHP, if it has entered the game, **do not object** within 30 days of receipt of an adequately documented determination, **then** the Agency Official's responsibilities under Section 106 are fulfilled. She may then **retire from play**, having gained her desired payoff of a prompt and successfully completed Section 106 review.

If the Agency Official **determines** that there is at least one Historic Property that may be affected by the Undertaking, or the SHPO/THPO or the ACHP **objects** to the Agency Official's finding that there are no such properties, **then** the Agency Official **notifies** all players, including Indian tribes or Native Hawaiian organizations, **invites** their views on the effects, and **assesses** adverse effects (move to the next round of the game).

Analysis

This second round of the game is very important because there is a great deal at stake for all players. **If** the Agency Official succeeds in convincing the other players that no Historic Properties are located within the Undertaking's Area of Potential Effects, or, there are Historic Properties that her Undertaking will have no effect upon whatsoever,

then she can promptly retire from the game, having successfully completed Section 106 review. The other players, therefore, will be on their guard to make sure they have received an administratively complete documentation package from her that accurately assesses any known Cultural Resources located within the APE for their National Register eligibility.

During this round of the game, based upon their own goals and strategies, players sometimes disagree concerning the size and scope of the APE. In addition, they sometimes disagree over the 'facts' contained within the Agency Official's determination documentation package. In such instances, they may 'raise' by requesting the preparation of additional documents, survey reports, etc. and/or they may propose to make a site visit to verify the 'facts on the ground'. **If** certain players remain dis-satisfied with the results of the Agency Official's determination, **then** they may 'raise' through a petition to the SHPO or the ACHP to invoke a formal determination of eligibility from the Keeper of the National Register of Historic Places. Play cannot end, or even continue to the next round of the game until the issue of National Register eligibility has been resolved.

If there is consensus, either that no Historic Properties are located within the APE or the Undertaking will not affect any known Historic Properties in any way, **then** play ends. **If** there is consensus that there are Historic Properties, or the Keeper so rules, **then** play moves to the next round.

Next Round Play By Play

Midgame (Reaction) / Assessment of Adverse Effects / 36 CFR 800.5

During this third Section 106 review round, the Agency Official **reacts** to the consultation she has received from the other players that Historic Properties exist within her APE, and then **'bids' an assessment of the effects** of her Undertaking upon those identified Historic Properties. These effects can be either benign, neutral, or adverse, depending upon the nature of the Undertaking, its scope, or the qualities of the Historic Property that make it National Register eligible. She uses the Criteria of Adverse Effect found at 36 CFR 800.5 to inform her findings of project-related effects. She does so **in consultation** with the SHPO/THPO and any Indian tribe or Native Hawaiian organization that attaches religious and cultural significance to identified Historic Properties. She also **considers** any views concerning such effects that have been provided by other players, including the public.

At the end of her review process, The Agency Official, in consultation with the SHPO/THPO, may **'bid' a finding of "no adverse effect"** when the Undertaking's effects do not meet the Criteria of Adverse Effect or she may **'bid' an agreement to modify the original Undertaking or impose conditions upon it to avoid adverse effect.**

Endgame

If the Agency Official **'bids' a finding of "no adverse effect"**, **then** she **notifies** all the other players and **provides** them with a specified set of documents that support her finding. The SHPO/THPO has 30 days from receipt to review the finding **('pass', 'call', 'raise')**. Unless the ACHP is reviewing the finding, the Agency

Official may **retire** from the game successfully and proceed with the Undertaking **if** the SHPO/THPO **agrees** with her finding or **withholds comment**. Failure of the SHPO/THPO to respond **('pass')** within 30 days from receipt of the finding is considered agreement with the finding. In this event, the Agency Official may **retire** from the game and proceed with the Undertaking, having successfully completed the process.

If any player, other than the public, **disagrees with** her finding within the 30-day review period, **then** that player must **specify** the reasons for disagreeing with her finding. The Agency Official shall either **consult** with the objecting player to resolve the disagreement, or **request** the ACHP to review her finding. **If** this consultation produces no resolution to the disagreement, or **if** the Agency Official finds an adverse effect on her own, **then** the Agency Official **consults** further with the other players to resolve the adverse effect (moves to the final round of the game).

Analysis

The Agency Official's reaction to the responses of the other players, her assessment of project effects upon Historic Properties, and her finding of either no adverse effect or adverse effect all generate some of the most spirited play in the entire game. During this third round, the other players test their strategies against those of the Agency Official who simply wants to get on with her Undertaking. Other players, such as the ACHP, and players with an abiding interest in historic preservation, and even the SHPO, whose goal is to provide the best advice and assistance on the correctness of her finding, will be testing and re-testing the validity of her finding; especially **if** it is one of "no adverse effect." On the other hand, players such as applicants for the particular type of Federal assistance under review, affected property owners who would benefit from the currently proposed Undertaking financially or otherwise, and representatives of local government whose goals coincide with 'growth and jobs' will be supporting the Agency Official's finding just as strongly.

Possible Formal Consulting Parties Meeting

At this point, a dis-satisfied Agency Official or Consulting Party may **petition** for a Formal Consulting Parties Meeting to provide a forum for a face-to-face discussion and resolution of that player's contentious issues. At this Meeting, the Agency Official and the other players will 'bid' their individual and collective goals and use those strategies they believe will win them the best positive payoffs.

Last Round / Showdown Play By Play

Resolution, Endgame / Resolution of Adverse Effects / 36 CFR 800.6

If, on the other hand, the players in this round reach consensus that there is "no adverse effect" or a "conditional no adverse effect" exists, **then** the Agency Official retires having successfully completed the process. However, **if** the end of play in this round results in a consensus finding of "adverse effect", **then** the Agency Official and the other players move to the final round of the game.

During this final Section 106 review round, the Agency Official **continues to consult** with the other players while **assessing**

SECTION 106 AND GAME THEORY

alternatives to her Undertaking that would avoid, minimize, or mitigate project-related adverse effects to Historic Properties. She first **examines** avoidance alternatives, then minimization alternatives, and then mitigation alternatives as a last resort. Any alternatives she examines *must be prudent and feasible and must meet the purpose and need of the Undertaking*.

In consultation with the SHPO/THPO and any Indian tribe or Native Hawaiian organization that attaches religious and cultural significance to identified Historic Properties, the Agency Official makes a good faith effort to consider any views concerning the avoidance, minimization, or mitigation of the effects that have been provided by other players.

At the end of her review process, the Agency Official, in consultation with the SHPO/THPO, may **'bid'**:

- a finding of no adverse effect due to a consensus-reached avoidance alternative to the originally-bid Undertaking, or
- a finding of conditional no adverse effect due to a consensus-reached re-design of the Undertaking that minimizes adverse effect, or
- a finding that there are no prudent or feasible alternatives that support the Undertaking's purpose and need due to a consensus-reached finding

If consensus among the players **opts for mitigation, then** the Agency Official **consults** with the SHPO/THPO, affected tribe, and perhaps an applicant for Federal assistance or some other player to **seek agreement** on the best way the adverse effect may be mitigated. The Agency Official **memorializes** this consensus in a Memorandum of Agreement (MOA). This MOA, once executed by signatories and invited signatories concludes the Section 106 review game successfully.

Analysis

In a certain few Section 106 reviews, where mitigation is the only viable option, players who have become disenchanted with the course of events up to that point tend to confront each other more harshly during this last round of game play than during any previous round. A large part of the reason for this heightened contentiousness lies with the fact that Step Four is the 'final showdown' round or 'final end game'. Disputatious players understand this to mean there will soon be a 'winner-take-all' resolution of the case. Either the Agency Official wins outright (the mitigated Undertaking proceeds in some form), or dis-satisfied players challenge the manner of the Agency Official's game play and petition the ACHP to review the case's procedure. This petitioning and the ACHP's subsequent procedural review may protract the game into extra, time-and-money-devouring rounds. Meanwhile, the Undertaking languishes and identified Historic Properties remain threatened.

Summing Up

Notwithstanding certain contentious end game conflicts, the overwhelming majority of Section 106 reviews end successfully with positive payoffs being realized by all players. Even so, those involved in the process must be prepared for confrontation among the players to occur at any point in a protracted Section 106 review. The intensity of conflict tends to escalate as players near the end of each round and becomes most pronounced at the nominal conclusion of Step Four.

SECTION 106 AND GAME THEORY

THE NASH EQUILIBRIUM

"Creating an undesired stalemate is the height of stupidity"
- *Unknown Source*

"Creating a desirable stalemate is the height of good sense"
- *Joe Garrison*

In his very useful book, *Game Theory 101, The Complete Textbook*, William Spaniel devotes a great deal of space to a discussion of what Game Theorists refer to as the 'Nash Equilibrium'. It is billed as a solution concept appropriate for a *non-cooperative game* involving two or more players. Therefore, it is worth study by those who occasionally find themselves involved in protracted Section 106 review games that have become non-cooperative.

As stated above, a game of Section 106 review can sometimes become non-cooperative and even confrontational, especially if the game play is protracted and the various players become impatient, obstinate, and inflexible in the employment of their strategies as they attempt to attain their respective unilateral goals. What ensues is comparable to a 'Nash Equilibrium'.

The 'Nash Equilibrium' is named after John Forbes Nash, Jr., who first described it in his 1951 article "Non-Cooperative Games" (BTW, Nash was awarded the Nobel Prize in Economics in 1994, so he is certainly a man to be listened to on this subject). A Nash Equilibrium is achieved when competing players have all chosen strategies by which they try to attain their goals (payoffs), where no individual player believes he or she has anything to gain by changing his or her own strategy *so long as the other players do not change their own strategies*.

SECTION 106 AND GAME THEORY

In any game of Section 106 review, one can expect each participant to open play with a strategy he or she assumes will attain the highest desired payoff for that player at the end of that particular Step. **If** each player bases that strategy solely upon what he or she considers his or her own best self-interest without any regard for the goals and strategies of the other players, **then** conflict and confrontation are likely to ensue.

EXAMPLE: For argument's sake, let's say that, pressed for time and short of funds, an Agency Official's opening Step Two strategy is to risk confrontation with the SHPO by submitting only the barest documentation in support of her determination that her Undertaking's APE contains no Historic Properties. **If** the SHPO's placeholder challenge 'bid' of "potential adverse effect" in response to her "no Historic Properties" 'bid' reflects his consistent strategy of requiring full support documentation before making an informed response to an Agency Official's determination, and the Agency Official knows that this, the SHPO's strategy, is set in stone through previous experience with him, she must **then** ask herself, would she benefit by changing her own strategy by preparing full documentation. She will weigh the consequences associated with the additional time and money spent in preparing satisfactory documentation versus the time and money lost in confronting the SHPO in hopes of forcing him to change his own strategy. **If** she decides to acquiesce and prepare appropriate documentation, **then** her revised strategy is no longer in Nash Equilibrium. However, **if** she decides that her best decision is not to switch strategies (or she is indifferent between switching and not) and the SHPO prefers to maintain his strategy not to reach consensus with her based on the unacceptable level of documentation she has submitted, **then** a Nash Equilibrium exists.

To me, this is just another name for 'stalemate', and it has unfortunate consequences in Section 106 review.

The Agency Official and the SHPO are in Nash Equilibrium when the Agency Official truly believes she is making the best decision she can, taking into account the SHPO's decision while the SHPO's decision remains unchanged. Remember that a large part of her final decision rests with the fact that her available time for preparing an administratively complete environmental review document is extremely limited as are her funds for preparing supporting documentation.

The SHPO also truly believes he is making the best decision he can, based upon his regulatory mandate to make an informed response to the Agency Official's 'bid', while taking into account the Agency Official's decision while the Agency Official's decision remains unchanged. Remember that the SHPO is responsible for reviewing the proposed Undertakings of a vast number of Federal agencies and therefore believes he must maintain a uniform consistency in the level of support documentation he deems necessary to securing informed SHPO determinations.

All other participants in this particular Section 106 review game will find themselves in Nash Equilibrium when each one believes he or she is making the best decision possible, taking into account the decisions of the others in the game as long as the other participants' decisions remains unchanged. So long as the Agency Official, SHPO, and the other participants cling to their erstwhile strategies and goals, no one will see any reason to move the game beyond Nash Equilibrium.

Therefore, it will likely end in stalemate, which means a failed and non-compliant review.

A close reading of that section of Presh Talwalkar's book that discusses this topic in detail will immediately confirm the impression that being stuck in such a Nash Equilibrium as the one here described is not a good thing for any of the players involved. Nor is it likely to result in any kind of a successful conclusion of the game. However, to give John Forbes Nash his due, we must concede that, in those games such as 'Brinkmanship', where rational participants *do not* desire a conclusion to the game (Armageddon), a Nash Equilibrium is not so bad, after all. Just ask T. C. Schelling with his MAD strategy that did so much to preclude a truly 'terminal' endgame.

Nonetheless, for our purposes, the resistance of both the Agency Official and the SHPO to changing their respective strategies and goals concerning the appropriate level of support documentation based upon the known strategies of the other players very likely will only cause this particular game of Section 106 review to become ever more confrontational.

Author's Note - In the July 27, 2016 issue of the "Urban Confessional" website, Benjamin Mathes' article "How to Listen When You Disagree: A Lesson from the Republican National Convention" offers a 'last ditch' recommendation for participants in any interaction where confrontation and dispute have arisen, and all sides are stuck in a Nash Equilibrium stalemate. Mathes writes, "When you find yourself in [stalemated] disagreement, just ask one question: ''Will you tell me your story''? In Section 106 review, as in any other game where cooperation may degenerate into confrontation, it is of paramount importance for participants to sense that, no matter the differences that have driven them into non-cooperation, they are all still considered to be 'good people' who came by their differences honestly.

Robert Axelrod, that eminent student of Game Theory, puts it this way, "Teach people to care about each other." Axelrod believes that, in the long run, any game depends for its success upon the mutuality of trust felt among the individual human beings who participate in it. According to Mathes, a very effective method for building and sustaining that trust among participants when faced with confrontation is to make this simple statement, "I'd love to know how you came to this point of view."

There is really only one way to break the deadlock of a Nash Equilibrium such as the one just described. Participants in Section 106 review must be committed to altering their strategies based upon their assessments of the true goals of other participants after asking Mathes' pivotal question. The SHPO must be willing to take the Agency Official's time and funding constraints into consideration, while the Agency Official must be willing to allocate sufficient time and money to match the SHPO's documentation requirements as closely as possible within reason. Only the natural give and take that results from continuing, interdependent, and flexible consultation between the two will create a conducive environment for change in both players.

Could this be the reason why a 'Red Phone' connecting Washington and Moscow was a key element in the 'MAD' strategy?

In this particular Section 106 review case, a reasonable compromise that breaks the Nash Equilibrium stalemate might involve an Agency Official/SHPO joint site visit to the Undertaking's APE where both players could discover whether Historic Properties did or did not exist within the project's impact area. In either case, it is more than likely that consensus on eligibility could be reached "on the spot" and the Agency Official's determination would either be vindicated or she would have to move on to Step Three, but be consoled by the notion that she could then expend her limited resources of time and funds on an assessment of project effect rather than National Register eligibility.

Game Theory offers rational players a number of additional effective strategies for breaking a Nash Equilibrium as well as other great lessons for preventing and resolving conflict. Read further to discover them.

PART FOUR: THE GREAT LESSONS

'SYMMETRY AND PARITY'

"Symmetry is what we see at a glance; based on the fact that there is no reason for any difference..."
- Blaise Pascal

"As to ethics, the parties seem to me as much on a parity as the pot and the kettle."
- Robert H. Jackson

In his revealing series of video lectures, Dr. Arthur T. Benjamin discourses extensively on two concepts central to Game Theory. These concepts have proved to be very useful when attempting to break a stalemated Nash Equilibrium. They are known as 'Symmetry' and 'Parity'.

Symmetry is defined as "similarity or exact correspondence between different things". Another definition emphasizes the **state of being symmetrical**; that is, corresponding in size, shape, and relative position to parts on opposite sides of a dividing line or median plane or about a center or axis. Symmetry is a **state of being** in balance and correspondence.

Parity is defined as "the state or condition of **becoming** equal". Another definition emphasizes the state of **becoming** equally odd or even as compared with another.

The key difference between the two concepts lies in the fact that **parity** is a state of **becoming** equal while **symmetry** is a state of **being** equal.

EXAMPLE: You come upon two trains sitting side by side in a railroad marshalling yard. The engines of both trains are parallel to each other. **If** both trains currently have the same number of box cars of the same size, **then** they have **symmetry**. **If** you stood in the space between the two trains and looked from both engines to both cabooses, **then** one train would correspond in size, shape, and relative position to the other train on the opposite side of your dividing line vantage point. In other words, they are 'even' with each other.

This is so because the marshalling yard foreman took a **set of actions** at some time in the past (**parity**) to arrange them so. **If** one train has one box car removed by the marshalling yard foreman, **then** it will become 'odd' with the other and there is no **symmetry**. **If** he removes a boxcar from the other train (**parity**), **then** he will restore **symmetry** to the two trains.

At first blush, these two words may seem to be nearly synonyms. However, they are not, as Dr. Benjamin makes quite plain. Once understood, both concepts become extremely valuable when one analyzes games with an eye to discovering winning strategies and breaking confrontational logjams.

SECTION 106 AND GAME THEORY

The Game Of NIM And Its Winning Strategy

In 1901, the highly-regarded mathematician, Charles Leonard Bouton, derived the complete mathematical strategy for winning the two-player game of NIM.

Author's Note - There are some who claim Bouton invented the game in order to derive its solution.

Bouton's derivation is of great importance to the history of modern Game Theory. One reason for its importance is that it became famous. By inference, it held out the possibility of creating similar mathematical derivations for wining other board games, card games, and puzzles. This possibility inspired a whole generation of Game Theorists such as Von Neumann. Their highly useful mathematical modeling has inspired still others whose work has been carried forward well into the Computer Age.

For those unfamiliar with the game, NIM is a 'Category Three' mathematical, 'take away', 'last mover wins' game of strategy in which two players take turns removing objects (coins, buttons, etc.) from two distinct 'heaps' (columns). At each turn, a player must remove at least one object. She may remove any number of objects provided they all come from the same heap.

In NIM, it is important to keep in mind that the person who makes the last move (i.e., who takes away the last object(s)) wins the game. Therefore, in that respect, NIM is analogous to Section 106 review; a last-mover-wins, Category Three game. This makes it quite amenable to analogous predictive analysis.

In NIM, if the opening player removes an asymmetrical number of objects from one heap, **then** the second 'player's' *best* chance to win would be to adopt a '**parity**' strategy, that is, to restore the size, shape,

SECTION 106 AND GAME THEORY

and relative position of game pieces on one side of the dividing line between the two heaps to that of game pieces on the opposite side of that line. Here is an example of a NIM board to illustrate the point

The Opening NIM Game Board

1 2
* *
* *
* *
* *
* *
  *
  *

Player A removes one game piece from heap 2.

1 2
* *
* *
* *
* *
* *
  *

SECTION 106 AND GAME THEORY

Player B **then** removes one game piece (**parity**) from heap 2, thereby making both heap 1 and heap 2 **symmetrical**.

```
1 2
* *
* *
* *
* *
* *
```

At this point, no matter how many game pieces Player A removes from whatever column, Player B can remove the same number of pieces (**parity**) from the other column until he is the last player able to move, and therefore wins.

PROOF

If Player A removes three game pieces from column 2...

```
1 2
* *
* *
*
*
*
```

SECTION 106 AND GAME THEORY

...Player B need only remove three game pieces (**parity**) from column 1.

```
1 2
* *
* *
```

By using a parity strategy to keep the game board symmetrically balanced by removing no more and no fewer than the number of pieces removed by Player A, Player B constantly returns the board to symmetry, thereby assuring his eventual win. No matter what Player A does from this point onward, Player B can use parity to return the board to symmetry until only one object remains on the board, which he takes to win. Here is the current NIM board...

```
1 2
* *
* *
```

If Player A removes one object, **then** Player removes one object. Player A must remove the last object in heal# 1, leaving Player B to win by removing the last object on the board from heap# 2.

Even **if** Player A removed both objects from heap# 1, **then** Player B still wins by removing both objects from heap# 2.

According to Dr. Benjamin, here is a distillation of Bouton's mathematical derivation for winning the game of NIM:

- "In an asymmetrical game such as NIM, either player can force a win, first by making it symmetrical, **then** by making each future move in parity with the moves of his opponent."

- "**If** a player is in a good (symmetrical) position, **then** all possible next moves of his opponent are going to be bad, either because he can retain symmetry or return to it by using parity."
- "From a bad (asymmetrical) position, there is always at least one move a player can make to make it a good position, because he can return the game board to symmetry, then use parity to force a win."
- "Even as the game of NIM grows in complexity, the rules of symmetry and parity still apply in analogous games."

Author's Note – In today's world of asymmetrical warfare, it would seem that conventional battle leaders could learn a great deal about attaining victory through an informed and discerning study of 'Symmetry and Parity'.

SECTION 106 REVIEW AND 'SYMMETRY AND PARITY'

"Extremes are Easy. Strive for Balance"
-Colin Wright

By using analogous predictive analysis, we can test our assertion that the applied rules of Symmetry and Parity pertain equally well to a game of Section 106 review and a game of NIM. Let Player A be the Agency Official or applicant for Federal assistance and let Player B be the SHPO. The opening Section 106 NIM board (Steps Two, Three, and Four) looks something like this....

SECTION 106 AND GAME THEORY

1	2	
*	*	Mitigation
*	*	Minimization
*	*	Avoidance
*	*	Adverse Effect
*	*	Conditional No Adverse Effect
*	*	No Adverse Effect
*	*	Historic Properties
*	*	No Historic Properties
*	*	Cultural Resources
*	*	No Cultural Resources
*	*	Area of Potential Effects

Player A opens the game by proposing an Area of Potential Effects in which no Cultural Resources or Historic Properties exist. She therefore removes all game pieces that represent everything between Area of Potential Effects and No Historic Properties.

SECTION 106 AND GAME THEORY

Now the game board looks like this...

```
1  2
*  *      Mitigation
*  *      Minimization
*  *      Avoidance
*  *      Adverse Effect
*  *      No Adverse Effect
*  *      Historic Properties
   *      No Historic Properties
   *      Cultural Resources
   *      No Cultural Resources
   *      Area of Potential Effects
```

At this point, the game is asymmetrical.

Player B can either agree or disagree with Player A's determinations. In either case, Player B returns the game to symmetry by using parity to resolve any outstanding issues that may have arisen having to do with Area of Potential Effects, Cultural Resources, and the determination of no Historic Properties affected. These parity moves may involve continued consultation, cultural resource surveys, site visits, consultation meetings, and so forth.

Now the game board looks like this...

```
1  2
*  *     Mitigation
*  *     Minimization
*  *     Avoidance
*  *     Adverse Effect
*  *     Conditional No Adverse Effect
*  *     No Adverse Effect
*  *     Historic Properties
         No Historic Properties
         Cultural Resources
         No Cultural Resources
         Area of Potential Effects
```

Through parity, the game board is symmetrical once more.

If after Player B has made certain moves that compel Player A to re-evaluate National Register eligibility, **then** Player A determines there *are* Historic Properties located within the APE that may be affected by the Federal Undertaking, and **then** she removes the game piece representing Historic Properties...

SECTION 106 AND GAME THEORY

```
1 2
* *      Mitigation
* *      Minimization
* *      Avoidance
* *      Adverse Effect
* *      No Adverse Effect
  *      Historic Properties
         No Historic Properties
         Cultural Resources
         No Cultural Resources
         Area of Potential Effects
```

...Player B can then use parity to return the game to symmetry by agreeing with Player A.

```
1 2
* *      Mitigation
* *      Minimization
* *      Avoidance
* *      Adverse Effect
* *      No Adverse Effect
         Historic Properties
         No Historic Properties
         Cultural Resources
         No Cultural Resources
         Area of Potential Effects
```

From this point onward, Player B can force a win by using parity to return the game board to symmetry each time Player A chooses an asymmetrical move. No matter where consultation ends, up to and including mitigation of adverse effect, where the SHPO is the *last signatory* on a Memorandum of Agreement, Player B will be the last player to move, and therefore the winner. This is true unless Player A throws over the rules altogether and retires from the game in a state of non-compliance.

The object here is for the winning player making the last move of the game to have preserved Symmetry and Parity throughout. **If** the Agency Official makes cooperative moves that stay within the rules laid down by 36 CFR 800, **then** the SHPO responds cooperatively (parity), returning the game board to symmetry. **If** the Agency Official makes a non-cooperative move, **then** the SHPO employs 'reciprocity' eventually to return the game board to symmetry (more later on reciprocity). The Agency Official always has the power of the first move. However, the SHPO has the power of 'Symmetry and Parity'.

SPECIFIC LESSONS LEARNED FROM PROFESSOR ARTHUR T. BENJAMIN

"Simplicity, simplicity, simplicity! I say, let your affairs be as two or three, and not a hundred or a thousand..."
- *Henry David Thoreau*

By way of counterpoint to Professor Ridgley's skepticism about the usefulness of Game Theory in a complex and chancy world, let's examine a few of Professor Benjamin's simple and positive Game Theory lessons.

SECTION 106 AND GAME THEORY

Lesson# 1: Use The 1/3 Bluff Formula

Players in a nuanced or complex Section 106 review game occasionally find themselves participating in a Formal Consulting Parties Meeting. Each will have already decided upon a particular opening strategy designed to resolve matters in her favor. Each is required by the consultative rules of the game to exercise that opening strategy interdependently with the other players during the early stages of the Meeting.

Let us assume one of the participant's strategies involves bluffing; that is, bragging a strong case for a determination of eligibility despite a weak 'hand' due to the lack of verifiable supporting documentation. Through the challenges of certain other participants, this player suddenly become aware that her bluffing strategy *may* fail, thus weakening her chances of attaining her payoff goal. In game terms, she perceives there is a good chance her bluff is about to be 'called'.

Professor Benjamin recommends that she should still continue to bluff in 1/3 of the Formal Consulting Party Meetings she attends in hopes that the bluff will succeed, even despite the actions of other players. He shares hard statistical evidence to support this recommendation.

As a caveat, Benjamin also states that a bluffing player should be prepared to retire from the game ('fold') and lose outright 2/3 of the time.

Professor Benjamin suggests that a 1/3 bluff / 2/3-fold grand strategy will succeed over the long haul in attaining the majority of those payoff goals *that were amenable to being acquired by bluffing*. Since bluffing is a perfectly acceptable strategy in Section 106 review, Professor Benjamin's advice is worth taking (See my up-coming book on Section 106 and Poker to learn more about both the legitimacy of and the techniques of bluffing.).

Lesson# 2: Thwart Irrational Players And Contested Games

Professor Ridgely sagely warns us that irrational participants may attempt to use the rules of a game like Section 106 review to ferret out and exploit the weaknesses of other players while preventing them from finding and exploiting their own. One of the reasons I wrote this book was to use the experience of writing it as a test bench to assess the value of modern Game Theory's methods as a possible foil in such needlessly non-cooperative Section 106 review games. I asked myself, were Game Theory's lessons useful in cases where opponents' goals were diametrically opposed to those of others? In these types of 'contested' games, Professor Benjamin states unequivocally that the better part of wisdom is for the principal players – the Agency Official and the SHPO -- to demand that all other participants play strictly by the rules while at the same time preventing those rules from being used to subvert the process.

Despite Professor Ridgley's admonitions about irrational players and their power to thwart the success of their rational opponents, Professor Benjamin asserts that, in all but a tiny fraction of cases, the strategies and goals of irrational players will eventually fail them, and rational game play can then continue uninterrupted.

Lesson# 3: Break It Down

Professor Benjamin makes a very constructive observation when he states, "**If** you cannot solve the big game, **then** solve as many of the game's component parts as you can". By this he means that **if** the game board becomes too complicated or nuanced for a player to formulate and implement a winning overall strategy, **then** that player should mentally divide the game board into manageable segments and attempt to devise strategies that will allow him to attain a positive payoff in each segment.

When rational and intelligent players of a Section 106 review game are faced with a situation too complex or nuanced for them to resolve easily, it would be well for them to divide that complex state of affairs into manageable segments and solve as many of those segments as possible.

EXAMPLE: An Undertaking's APE contains three National Register eligible historic districts, each encompassing at least one hundred contributing buildings. Assessing project-related effects upon each one of these contributing buildings would be complicated, time-consuming, and prohibitively expensive for the Agency Official. Taking into account this complexity and cost, participants in the Section 106 review agree to limit the Agency Official's effect assessment to only those contributing buildings within sight or sound of the Undertaking. Furthermore, various participants contribute whatever information they already possess about those selected buildings, thus further reducing complexity and cost to the Agency Official. The result is a reasonable assessment sanctioned by interdependent consultation and readily supported by all participants.

Facilitated Section 106 review dispute resolution scenarios usually resolve themselves in just this fashion.

Lesson# 4: Work Backwards

Professor Benjamin proposes that game players who win most of the games they play tend to work backwards from their ultimate payoff goal by using what mathematicians refer to as 'retrograde analysis'.

EXAMPLE: If an Agency Official's ultimate goal is to determine that there are no Historic Properties affected within her APE, **then** she should work backwards from that goal, using due diligence properly to identify and evaluate every Cultural Resource located within the APE; and backwards even further to make sure her APE is correctly bounded. That way, **if** she does attain her goal, **then** it will be nearly impossible for other participants to challenge her determination of "no Historic Properties affected" successfully.

However, **if** due diligence, consultation, and proper evaluation determine the existence of at least one Historic Property inside her APE, **then** the Agency Official must be willing to move cooperatively on to the next Step of play. This is also true if an Agency Official who is aware of a Historic Property within her APE has stated an ultimate goal of "no adverse effect" or one who is aware of adverse effect who states her ultimate goal as "no prudent or feasible alternatives" that will avoid or minimize that adverse effect.

SHPO's and other Consulting Parties must also work backwards from their own ultimate goals with due diligence to ensure they can counter any challenges successfully.

Lesson# 5: Reject The 'Greedy' Strategy.

Professor Benjamin maintains that players who pursue a 'greedy' strategy take the big risk of defeating themselves at showdown. For him, the best game gratification is deferred gratification.

To Dr. Benjamin, a 'greedy' strategy is a type in which a participant in a game comes to the table always expecting immediate agreement with all of his stated goals from the other players, without ever allowing himself to become aware of the stated goals of those other participants. Such a strategy is quite likely to be off putting to the other players who will tend to react negatively even though they might themselves agree with some or even all of the 'greedy' participant's goals.

EXAMPLE: An Agency Official whose 'greedy' strategy is always to press for a speedy "no Historic Properties affected" concurrence from the SHPO and other Consulting Parties eventually risks a 'knee jerk' reaction from them that calls for increasingly detailed support documentation even if it is obvious that the particular Undertaking under current review has no potential whatsoever to affect Historic Properties. This is especially true if the Agency Official never expresses any desire to understand or empathize with SHPO and Consulting Party goals.

Professor Benjamin uses mathematical modeling in simple games such as Solitaire to demonstrate that the best way for a player to win over time is to practice deliberation and discernment until he can be assured of attaining his payoff goals. This deferral strategy also allows time for players to learn about the goals of other players and to form like-minded alliances.

A VINDICATION OF COOPERATION IN GAME THEORY: ROBERT AXELROD

"Competition has been shown to be useful up to a certain point and no further, but cooperation, which is the thing we must strive for today, begins where competition leaves off."
- Franklin D. Roosevelt

There has been much discussion so far in this book about cooperation versus competition. Discerning readers have good reason to believe that modern Game Theory has its share of proponents who believe strongly that a player's ultimate best interest decision is to cooperate with other players. However, I am obliged to point out that there are still others within the discipline who support the notion just as strongly that a player's ultimate best interest decision is to compete against other players. The struggle between these two contending views has troubled Game Theorists almost from the beginning and that struggle continues today.

Right now, a whole host of Game Theory books with titles such as: *Game Theory: Analysis of Conflict, The Art of Strategy: A Game Theorist's Guide to Success in Business and Life, Game Theory: How to Make Better Decisions Every Day Using Game Theory to Get Everything You Always Wanted,* and *Game Theory: Toolkit and Workbook for Defense Analysis Students* line bookstore shelves row on row, vying with each other for the attention of the serious reader whose personal best goal is to win, win, win and whose basic assumptions tie 'winning' to 'competing'.

EXAMPLE: When proposing the best utility in the 'Prisoner's Dilemma' game, William Spaniel asserts that, since it is *obvious* that each prisoner cares only about his own time in jail, the best utility for either is to confess to the crime ASAP and go free, even though doing so ensures his partner in crime's 'payoff' is a long jail term.

I am not certain that Mr. Spaniel is correct, although many in the discipline tend to agree with him. As one who has practiced in the field of environmental review for more than thirty years, I must confess that Mr. Spaniel's self-interest assumption about the prisoners in this scenario is not all that obvious to me. I have been a participant in many, many Section 106 review cases where participants chose to sacrificed their own self-interest to a commonly-agreed-upon endgame.

Let us suppose for a moment that the two prisoners facing this iconic Game Theory dilemma are brothers. Perhaps under these peculiar circumstances Mr. Spaniel might be persuaded to re-think his assumption; or perhaps not. In any case, it would seem that, at least inside the MBA classrooms of our nation's major universities, confrontation and defection have won this decade's Game Theory Seal of Approval.

However, a number of prominent Game Theorists were not and still are not convinced that confrontation wins. As far back as the early 1980s, computers had become sufficiently powerful so that discerning Game Theorists like Robert Axelrod could harness their astounding computational power in an attempt to winnow out the final solution to the conundrum of cooperation versus competition. In true Game Theory style, Axelrod (Professor of Political Science and Public Policy at the University of Michigan) arranged a computer competition, pitting some of the world's foremost Game Theorists against each other. Like Spaniel, Axelrod used our old friend, the iconic 'Prisoner's Dilemma' trope, as his test bench. He knew that many members of the collective of reputable Game Theorists he had invited to participate in his competition had been using this game to test their own pet formulas ever since it had been introduced in the early 1950s, and so were quite familiar with it.

In 1984, Axelrod asked his Game Theory colleagues to act as contestants in this tournament. They would compete by submitting algorithms supporting their best research reasoning concerning the following two simple propositions:

1) if and when should one of the Prisoners **cooperate** by not 'ratting on' his cohort in crime, while still serving his own best interest?
2) if and when would it be in his own best interest to **compete** ('defect') by implicating his co-criminal in the crime before that person decided to do the same thing to him?

Each strategy was paired with each other strategy for 200 iterations of the Prisoner's Dilemma game, and scored on the total points accumulated through the tournament.

The Game Theorists who submitted a whopping sixty-two entries (some quite complex) represented a wide range of academic disciplines and a healthy scattering of nations from around the globe. Axelrod analyzed all entries carefully, then showcased the winning algorithm in his seminal book, *The Evolution of Cooperation*, (Basic Books, 1989).

The winning entry was submitted by Anatol Rapoport (May 22, 1911–January 20, 2007), then at the University of Toronto. Rapoport's winning strategy may be summarized quite neatly in that timeworn kids' way for dealing with disputes on the playground; 'Tit for Tat'. Axelrod held a second tournament to see if anyone could find a better strategy. 'Tit for Tat' won again!

The Strategy Of 'Tit For Tat'

Simply stated, 'Tit for Tat' is an effective strategy that begins any game with an opening 'bid' of either cooperation or confrontation. Thereafter, the player using this strategy does exactly what his opposite number did in the previous round.

Rapoport seems to be saying that, in a 'Tit for Tat' scenario, it is never in the interest of either Prisoner to defect upon his co-Prisoner so long as a mutuality of positive past experience, or the close ties of kinship, or some other rational mutuality of interest binds them together toward a common goal. Admittedly, unalloyed self-interest alone would always compel one Prisoner to defect, but Axelrod argues that there is no such thing as unalloyed personal self-interest among rational players. An un-cooperative bid is to be met with un-cooperation, not as a competitive challenge but as a "wake-up call" that cooperation among players is the best strategy for all to use to attain their highest payoffs.

For me, Anatol Rapoport's formulation of 'Tit for Tat' as a mathematically provable best strategy offers a robust vindication of the notion of cooperation supported by the art/science of Game Theory. That vindication greatly magnifies its utility in the area of conflict resolution.

In terms of Section 106 review, here is an example for you to read and contemplate.

EXAMPLE: Our first Agency Official, who has contributed to a long-standing and harmonious relationship with the SHPO 'bids' a cooperative review request that meets all the regulatory requirements of Steps One and Two. In his turn, the SHPO *promptly* 'bids' consensus and concurs cooperatively with the Agency Official's determination.

Our second Agency Official, either unfamiliar with the regulatory requirements or disdainful of them, 'bids' a review request with the bare minimum of support documentation in a vague and un-cooperative attempt to respond to Steps One and Two. In his turn, the SHPO *promptly* 'bids' an un-cooperative and detailed request for additional documentation needed to satisfy the process's regulatory requirements.

This is 'Tit for Tat' in a nutshell. Agency Official cooperation is *immediately* met with SHPO/THPO cooperation, just as it is immediately met with handshakes between two buddies during a Fourth Grade recess period. Agency Official non-cooperation is *immediately* met with SHPO/THPO non-cooperation, just as it is immediately met between a bully and his pugnacious target during that same recess period. Admittedly, the SHPO/THPO makes his non-cooperative response in the sincere hope that it will encourage the rational Agency Official to return to a cooperative posture so that the process may continue smoothly and promptly toward compliant completion.

'Tit For Tat' And 'Symmetry And Parity'

Those who have read discerningly up to this point will have surmised correctly that Rapoport's 'Tit for Tat' strategy sounds very much like Professor Benjamin's own winning strategy of 'Symmetry and Parity'. A 'bid' in symmetry (even) is met with a parity 'bid' (even) that returns the board to symmetry while an asymmetry 'bid' (odd) is also met with a parity 'bid' (odd) that also returns the board to symmetry. In either case, the second mover will eventually win.

SECTION 106 AND GAME THEORY

USING THE 'TIT FOR TAT' STRATEGY

"The way to work with a bully is to take the ball and go home. First time, every time. When there's no ball, there's no game. Bullies hate that."

- Seth Godin

In Section 106 review, the 'Tit for Tat' strategy proceeds like this:

EXAMPLE: We launch Step Two of a certain Section 106 review game where all participants begin in a spirit of cooperation.

The Agency Official 'bids' a well-reasoned and well-documented review request to the SHPO/THPO in a spirit of cooperation. By way of clarification, this cooperative review request contains a detailed project narrative, offers a complete Consulting Parties list, defines a reasonable APE, identifies all known Cultural Resources, evaluates them with due diligence using the Criteria of Eligibility in consultation with the SHPO and other Consulting Parties, seeks comments from the public, forwards a determination to the SHPO that there are Historic Properties located within the APE, and speculates they might be affected by her Undertaking.

The SHPO/THPO's strategy is to respond cooperatively and *immediately* (within fifteen days or less) to the Agency Official's cooperative opening 'bid'. He reviews the Agency Official's request promptly, and forwards a speedy consensus "Historic Properties affected" concurrence to the Agency Official. At the end of this Step Two round of play, 'Tit for Tat' has succeeded as a strategy for all players. Cooperation has prevailed and an informed review where consensus carries the day will have allowed all players to move, if necessary, to the next round promptly.

It is now necessary to move to the Step Three round of play because the Agency Official and the SHPO have reached consensus that Historic Properties are located within the Undertaking's APE.

Suppose at this point, however, that the Agency Official becomes frantic due to a sudden, problematic, and unyieldingly tight construction schedule for her Undertaking imposed upon her from above by her managers. This compels her to put the Section 106 review of her project at risk by making only the most cursory assessment of project effects upon the identified National Register eligible Historic Property. Her decision to do this is non-cooperative because it is contrary to the rules of the game codified at 36 CFR 800. She has 'defected' from the loyalty she had shown for the process up to this point.

Furthermore, she compounds her non-cooperativeness with the Section 106 review process by stating formally in her second round 'bid' finding to the SHPO that there will be "no adverse effect" to the Historic Properties; a bid supported by only a shred of evidence culled from her skimpy documentation and buttressed by no consultative support at all from the other Consulting Parties with whom she obviously had not conferred.

At this point, the SHPO/THPO, *promptly* (within ten days of receipt), and applying his own 'Tit for Tat' strategy of doing exactly what his opposite player has just done, immediately 'raises' the Agency Official's non-cooperative 'bid' with a strongly worded request for more detailed effect assessment documentation in lieu of the Agency Official's submitted skimpy assessment. The SHPO also asks the Agency Official to seek and to document formal comment from other Consulting Parties.

The Agency Official views this SHPO response as non-cooperative, and she is obviously correct.

This round of play is now stymied in a state of mutual non-cooperation and a potentially unfortunate Nash Equilibrium is in the offing until and unless the Agency Official decides to adopt a more cooperative strategy by producing an administratively complete effects assessment prepared with due diligence. Ironically, once she has prepared it, this revised and complete effects assessment allows her to arrive exactly at her earlier conclusion of "no adverse effect".

This new, revised, and complete agency finding is supported by positive responses from other Consulting Parties and the Agency Official documents that support as an addendum to her revised submission.

Now that the Agency Official has returned to a cooperative strategy in harmony with the documentation requirements of 36 CFR 800, the SHPO/THPO, again employing the 'Tit for Tat' strategy, *immediately* (within 7 days), responds cooperatively with a consensus finding of "no adverse effect".

Parity has restored Symmetry, and the Agency Official has completed the Section 106 review of this Undertaking successfully and in compliance.

'Tit for Tat' meets cooperation with *immediate* cooperation, non-cooperation with *immediate* non-cooperation, and a return to cooperation with an *immediate* return to cooperation. It is a strategy just as profoundly effective among highly-intelligent and highly-educated Game Theorists as it always has been among elementary school children. Is anyone surprised? Recess is short, and playground arguments must be solved quickly!

'TIT FOR TAT' AND THE 'GRIM TRIGGER'

"Let us therefore make every effort to do what leads to peace and to mutual edification."
- *Romans 14:19 New International Version*

We know that 'Tit for Tat' and 'Symmetry and Parity' meet cooperation automatically with prompt cooperation and asymmetrical non-cooperation automatically with prompt non-cooperation in hopeful anticipation of a speedy return to cooperation. That hope springs from an awareness that rational players will readily understand the benefits of cooperation. After all, 'Tit for Tat' *is* a rational and highly practical dispute resolution method. Ask any fourth grader.

However, Dr. Stevens admits that, while it may be formulated to induce cooperation among players, Tit for Tat' and 'Symmetry and Parity' have the potential to automatically meet round after round of non-cooperation with round after round of non-cooperation. Even worse, 'Tit for Tat' can sometimes induce continuous and unrelenting non-cooperation even if the non-cooperative player has defected only once. Dr. Stevens refers to this knee jerk adherence to 'Tit for Tat' as the 'Grim Trigger'.

Author's Note - The term "Grim Trigger" was first used by James Friedman to describe this unforgiving non-cooperative strategy in a paper delivered in 1971.

To Dr. Stevens, and to many of his colleagues as well, the 'Grim Trigger is regarded as the least forgiving of retaliation strategies, because it *is* so automatic and so infinite. Carried to an extreme, 'Tit for Tat' holds out no hope whatsoever for any future return to cooperation among players.

Stevens also points out that confrontation upon confrontation upon confrontation is a strategy most often used by irrational players who are diametrically opposed to any process that fosters cooperation.

These irrational participants are of the kind that "will not take 'No' for an answer". Nor are they the type of participants who would benefit from Game Theory guidance. Therefore, at some point during highly-protracted games where confrontation is growing apace and 'Tit for Tat' is not accomplishing its purpose, that method should be set aside and another cooperation-inducing set of strategies should be substituted. These Include:
- Polling
- "Playing Chicken"
- Compromise
- Fact Finding
- Obeying the Rules

These strategies will be discussed in detail in my forthcoming book, *Conflict In Section 106 Review: Causes, Consequences, And Cures*.

Summary

Irrational players who attempt to use 'Tit for Tat' and 'Symmetry and Parity' for their own dishonorable and self-serving purposes should be strictly avoided if at all possible by anyone who understands the value for all participants of interdependent, flexible, and cooperative game play. This is as true in Section 106 review as it is in any other review process.

SECTION 106 AND GAME THEORY

'THE EVOLUTION OF COOPERATION'

"You don't play against opponents. You play against the game...."
- Bobby Knight

"If you are a leader or someone who works for the interest of a community, first make sure that you understand the interest of the people who make up that community. In this way, you will have a good chance of minimizing, perhaps, avoiding the us versus them mentality."
— Duop Chak Wuol

To counter-balance the dangers of the 'Grim Trigger," Robert Axelrod maintains that a spirit of cooperation among the rational participants in a game will evolve once it is made known to them that cooperation is their proven best long-term mutual strategy. However, Axelrod acknowledges that cooperation does not necessarily depend upon *all* players sharing that understanding. Axelrod argues that **If** only *one* player desires to promote cooperation among the other players, **then** chances are this player will succeed, at least in part.

Axelrod is no idealist. He would be the first to admit that, unlike the goddess Athena, a spirit of cooperation does not naturally spring full grown from the head of Game Theory's Zeus. At least one participant in each game must promote it, first within herself. Then she must work to create a game environment that promotes cooperation among all players.

The Cooperative Personal Environment

According to Axelrod, promoting the **spirit of cooperation in oneself** has four components:

1. Don't be envious

Since Section 106 review is not a 'zero sum' game where one player's positive payoff automatically requires another player's payoff to be equally negative, there is no reason to presume that a 'win' on the part of the Agency Official means a 'loss' for the SHPO/THPO, or vice versa. Therefore, a participant in Section 106 review who attempts to compare her rate of attaining her own desired goals against the rates of other players misses the point entirely. Far better for all participants to think in terms of whether, with some help, some other player, while attempting to play his hand, could be doing as well as that player herself is doing. So long as a player keeps to the simple strategy of 'Tit for Tat', she will "hold her own" and eventually extract a spirit of cooperation from the other rational players because such a spirit will eventually prove to be in their mutual self-interest.

2. Don't be the first player to 'defect'

The best strategy for ultimate success is the promotion of and the pro-active continuation of cooperation among all players. By the rules of 'Tit for Tat', defection is risky because the first non-cooperative player will gain nothing except immediate non-cooperation from the other players. Only a return to a strategy of cooperation will gain an immediate return to cooperation from the other players.

EXAMPLE: If an Agency Official or applicant 'opens' with a less-than-adequate review request, **then** she should not be surprised by an immediate 'raise' from the SHPO. Only by submitting adequate documentation in support of her determination or finding can an Agency Official or applicant legitimately expect a return to cooperation by the SHPO. As play progresses, cooperation will be met with cooperation automatically.

3. Reciprocate both cooperation and defection

A player should begin a round of Section 106 review in the spirit of cooperation and reciprocate it immediately each time it is received from any other player. Likewise, a player should immediately reciprocate non-cooperation if received from another player, trusting that such a response will motivate that rational player to cooperate in future.

Given the existence of the 'Grim Trigger', here is a useful rule of thumb; **if** a non-cooperative response does not result in an immediate return to cooperation, **then** begin to suspect irrationality on the part of the non-cooperative player.

4, Don't be too clever

As we have seen, a rational player must always keep in mind that other players are reacting to her strategies and modifying their own to suit the changing conditions of play. Therefore, a player who devises a strategy designed to confuse, obfuscate, or complicate matters will probably be reciprocated with confusion, obfuscation, and complication by the other players.

The Cooperative Game Environment

According to Axelrod, for a player to create a **game environment** that promotes a spirit of cooperation among all players she must call to mind and employ these five strategies:

1. Enlarge the shadow of the future

Axelrod contends that an environment of stability and mutual cooperation between two game participants can be assured over time if the future of the relationship between them is sufficiently important to them, relative to their relationship in the present.

This is certainly the case with Section 106 review. Federal agencies that plan projects, programs, and activities subject to Section 106 review are 'corporate' in that they exist continually with no realistic expectation that they will soon disappear. This condition is also true of SHPOs, THPOs, Tribes, and local governments. Admittedly, applicants for Federal assistance do come and go, but the types of funds, licenses, permits, and approvals being applied for by them remain available year after year. Therefore, SHPOs who wish to promote long-term cooperation with Federal agencies can enlarge the shadow of the future by acting in ways that cause their agency counterparts to place increasing value upon maintaining a cooperative relationship with them for the long term.

SHPOs can accomplish this feat most easily by responding promptly, cooperatively, and consistently to cooperative agency and applicant review requests and, sorry to say, also by responding immediately, consistently, and non-cooperatively to any agency acts of non-cooperation.

Irrespective of the game being played, "trust, but verify" is as true for both sides of an issue today as it was during the Cold War. Therefore, long-term relationships built upon mutual trust become fertile ground for promoting habits of scheduled commitment tracking among the participants, especially if both sides have instituted mutually-agreed-to protocols for submitting, reporting, and carrying out avoidance, minimization, or mitigation measures.

2. Change the payoff

A much-hoped-for positive payoff for an Agency Official in the game of Section 106 review is consensus from the SHPO/THPO concerning all her determinations and findings. This is the 'steak' she hopes to find on her plate at the successful conclusion of each Section 106 case review. SHPO's who can legitimately reach such consensus within the rules set down at 36 CFR 800 should most certainly do so. However, *when* they do so will change the value of the Agency Official's payoff in positive ways that promote future cooperation.

The 36 CFR 800 Regulation allows 30 days for SHPO response to each review request. More than a few SHPOs will accommodate themselves to routinely taking the full 30 days, or even longer, or even much longer. Some other and more discerning ones, however, have made it a core policy to respond within a much shorter period, being well aware that time is money with Federal Undertakings subject to Section 106 review. This policy of expedited review and comment should be looked upon as the 'sizzle' on the Agency Official's steak that makes it much more enticing for her to return repeatedly and happily to the Section 106 review game.

3. Teach people to care about each other

It may surprise neophytes to the game to discover that Section 106 review is a very 'personal' business. To an astounding degree, this game depends for its success upon the mutuality of trust felt among the individual human beings who participate in it. The more SHPOs provide Agency Officials and applicants with the 'personal touch' of expedited reviews, consistent reviews, reasonableness of expectations concerning appropriate levels of documentation, access to site file information that is free of charge, and prompt accommodation to their requests for appointments, site visits, meetings, etc., the more there is an assurance of mutual high-value payoff. This trust will be shared in positive ways that promote long-term cooperation.

4. Teach reciprocity

Within the realm of Game Theory, the state of reciprocity encompasses the mutual exchange of rights, privileges, and obligations among players in a game. Reciprocity is the context in which the 'Tit for Tat' strategy has been mathematically proven. For this reason, it is among the best as well as among the simplest means of attaining the highest long-term payoffs for all players. **If** a participant 'bids' cooperation within the context of a mutual exchange of rights, privileges, and obligations between players, **then** cooperation will automatically be reciprocated. She has the right to expect cooperation as a privilege mutually shared, and she has an obligation to reciprocate cooperation with cooperation.

Special emphasis must be placed on the *immediacy* of the cooperative response. Anyone who has ever house-trained a puppy knows it does no good to rub its nose in cold pee. In any case, SHPO responses must be immediate in order for them to 'take'. An intelligent, rational Agency Official or applicant who submits correct, appropriate, and informative documentation in support of a rational determination or finding must receive as close to an immediate SHPO response of consensus as is possible. This imminence of a cooperative response fosters a state of continued cooperation from the Agency Official.

Likewise, an Agency Official or applicant who submits less than adequate documentation, or whose determination or finding is clearly at variance with the facts of the case, must receive an immediate, non-cooperative response that states unequivocally that additional or better documentation is required or a more discerning determination or finding must be submitted. The immediacy of a negative response from the SHPO, even though non-cooperative, still has a somewhat positive effect because it allows the Agency Official sufficient additional time to correct the flaws in her documentation or re-assess her determination or finding.

5. Improve recognition abilities

There are certain instances in Section 106 review where positive frameworks of cooperation between Agency Officials and SHPOs, erected painstakingly over a period of years, have suddenly been threatened with dissolution by one instance of non-cooperation on the part of one or the other of the participants. Ties of human trust that have bound cooperative game play tightly together for years suddenly seem to be cut.

It is at these uncharacteristically non-cooperative junctures when both sides must step back, re-assess, and strive to sharpen their former recognition abilities of one another. They need to ask, 'What external influences beyond the control of a normally-cooperative participant may be causing him unexpectedly to act non-cooperatively'. Can a reactive and non-cooperative 'Tit for Tat' response be softened in some way that allows for and even encourages the possibility of a return to the former state of cooperation? Can both sides avoid Brinkmanship? (See Cuban Missile Crisis)

Be advised. There is nothing whatsoever that violates the rules of Section 106 review in the notion of 'cutting some slack' for a normally cooperative player who has been aberrantly non-cooperative. Doing so at the right time may go far to avoid the risk of a 'Grim Trigger'.

THE MOST IMPORTANT LESSON

"If you want to be incrementally better: be competitive. If you want to be exponentially better: be cooperative."
- *Unknown Source*

The most important lesson Robert Axelrod has taught those of us in the chaos abatement business is that cooperation among rational players is mathematically more likely than competition to generate sustainable goals and attain rewarding payoffs for all. Almost 60 years of research and formulation of the mathematical 'rules' that govern rational game play demonstrate the soundness of this lesson. Even in those instances when communication among players is limited and the universe of possible goals is confined, cooperation remains the best strategy. Furthermore, even after a protracted game has devolved into confrontation and recrimination, a mutual agreement to return to cooperation remains the best strategy for all participants. An occasion for bitterness becomes an opportunity for betterment whenever the participant who brings his "hard feelings" to the consultation table is met with a spirit of common humanity and cooperation.

If a specific Section 106 review game has undergone many re-matches spread over a considerable period of time, **then** the initially strong sense of cooperation that was shared among the players will naturally tend to have eroded somewhat. Even so, Agency Officials who orchestrate Section 106 review games with many re-matches and the SHPOs who assist, advise, and cooperate with them can counteract this erosion to a measurable extent by encouraging a sustained high level of communication among the players. Human-centered consultation both encourages and re-invigorates cooperation.

Seasoned participants in Section 106 review who consult continually will not need to wonder all that much about what the other rational players in the game desire or are planning to do. We all know that the universe of goals and strategies is rather restricted by the rules of the game. Blessedly, communication in the form of interdependent, flexible, and frequent consultation among the various participants in Section 106 review is not restricted at all. It runs throughout the entire process and is central to the concept of "taking into account".

OVER THE LONG HAUL

"Reciprocal accountability, or criticism [is] the only known antidote to error."
- *David Brin*

Here are some 'home truths' to keep in mind as you re-assess Game Theory as a possible method for resolving or eliminating disputes in Section 106 review.

1) Let's be clear that 'Tit for Tat' *does depend upon* the promise of an eventual state of mutual cooperation in order to attain a final win/win for each of a game's participants. In 'Tit for Tat', non-cooperation is viewed as an aberration, to be met immediately with a non-

cooperative response with the assurance that such a non-cooperative response will automatically transform non-cooperation into cooperation among rational players. Whenever a momentarily non-cooperative yet rational player reverts to cooperation, the optimum response from the other participants is an immediate return to cooperation. 'Symmetry and Parity' are restored.

2) Game Theorists see all rational players as acting this way because of the power of mutual self-interest. They also admit that irrational players do not necessarily act this way because they will not abandon their perceived self-interest. In those instances, they state unequivocally that the tenets of Game theory do not apply.

3) Game Theory emphasizes the notion that those rational participants in a Section 106 review case who seek common ground with other participants through cooperative consultation that forms alliances are more likely over the long haul to attain their goals and receive the payoffs they desire. The more cooperation among the participants exists, the greater chance of mutual reward.

These core lessons of Game Theory align perfectly with successful Section 106 review only so long as the game is played by rational participants. Fortunately, the vast majority of Section 106 review participants are rational.

CHAOS THEORY

"In fact, the mere act of opening the box will determine the state of the cat, although in this case there were three determinate states the cat could be in: these being Alive, Dead, and Bloody Furious."
— Terry Pratchett

Before we leave the world of mathematical modeling altogether, I wish to take a short side trip into the realm of Chaos Theory because certain of its tenets have pertinence to Section 106 review. Chaos Theory is that branch of mathematics that deals with systems and processes whose behavior is highly sensitive to slight changes in initial conditions, so that small initial alterations in a system or process can give rise to strikingly different outcomes over time.

This aspect of Chaos Theory is referred to as 'Sensitivity to Initial Conditions'. It was identified by Edward Lorenz, who has been credited as its first experimenter in the early 1960s. Lorenz began the mathematical modeling that came to be known as Chaos Theory.

According to the Whatis.com website, Lorenz was a meteorologist tasked with running computerized equations to model and predict future weather conditions. "Having run a particular sequence, he decided to replicate it. Lorenz reentered the numbers from his printout, taken half-way through the sequence, and left it to run. What he found upon his return was, contrary to his expectations, these results were radically different from his first outcomes."

As it turned out, Lorenz had, in fact, not precisely entered an initial printout number (.506127) into his second run, but instead, the rounded figure of .506. Just this slight difference in the initial condition of the computer run as compared with its predecessor resulted in a *radically* different result for Lorenz.

Sensitivity To Initial Conditions

Chaos Theory postulates that an arbitrarily small initial change in the current path followed by either a projectile or a process within a system may lead to a significantly different future outcome as against the previous path. Experience gained from my review of over 70,000 Section 106 review cases demonstrates that all such reviews are, in fact, readily sensitive to initial conditions and therefore subject to Chaos Theory's analysis.

EXAMPLE: Initially, an Agency Official used the standard radius for protracting the circumference of the APE for a 250-foot- high lattice cellular tower (1.5 miles) to derive her APE. This was the APE she submitted to the SHPO for review and comment. She affirmed that within that APE lay three Cultural Resources and none of them were National Register eligible. After reviewing the submitted documentation, the SHPO concurred with the Agency Official's "no Historic Properties affected" determination, but requested that a revised report be submitted to his file with improved photographs of the project site.

Having concluded Section 106 review to her satisfaction, the Agency Official happily accommodated the SHPO and prepared a revised Cultural Resources report, but accidently changed the APE's circumference from 1.5 miles to 1.56 miles, due to a re-drawing error. When the SHPO's Review and Compliance Section staffers routinely reviewed the revised report, they suddenly discovered a National Register-listed property lying *inside* the Undertaking's revised APE.

The SHPO staffers' first reaction was "how could we have missed this"? Their second reaction was "now the Agency Official is obliged to move to Step Three and analyze potential project effect upon this newly-included Historic Property". Therefore, the Agency Official's protraction change, though very slight, altered the path of the review process significantly.

The Passage Of Time And The Decrease In Predictability

In Chaos Theory, a key consequence of sensitivity to initial conditions is that, if one begins with only a finite amount of information about the system or process (as is usually the case in the real world with games such as Section 106 review; games of incomplete information), then *beyond a certain time* the system will no longer be predictable. In our example, **if** sufficient time elapsed before the Agency Official's re-drawing mistake could be noticed and rectified, **then** her expected and correct determination of "no Historic Properties affected" outcome will have been significantly changed and she will have invested time, money, and effort analyzing project-related effects to a Historic Property that was actually located outside the boundary of her APE.

For a number of reasons, 36 CFR 800 requires SHPO responses to Agency Official determinations and findings to be delivered within 30 days or less. For our discussion, this time limit retains a level of predictability in Section 106 review outcomes that has proved to be most reliable. Much beyond this, however, and the predicted outcome of any specific review becomes increasingly un-reliable because of the process's sensitivity to initial conditions.

Valuable Guidance

Chaos Theory is replete with complex mathematical modeling and arcane terminology much of which borders on the unintelligible, at least for this writer. Nevertheless, the notion that Section 106 review outcomes can be radically changed by very slight alterations in the initial submitted review documentation, coupled with the notion that a trustworthy prediction of a Section 106 outcome becomes increasingly less trustworthy over time provide valuable cautionary guidance to anyone involved in the process.

INTERLUDE: PROMOTING COOPERATION DEFENDS THE PROCESS

"How you climb a mountain is more important than reaching the top."

- *Yvon Chouinard*

As seen repeatedly in this book, Game Theory teaches that cooperation is discernably more likely to resolve disputes arising from Section 106 review cases than is competition or confrontation. The roadmap to successful completion of the process, as codified at 36 CFR 800, points out numerous waypoints that shelter and encourage cooperation among the participants through the medium of interdependent, continuous, and flexible consultation. Following this roadmap has led to procedural success and compliance in innumerable Section 106 review cases over the past forty years. However, despite this impressive record of success, the entire Section 106 review process periodically comes under attack.

Certain elements within the historic preservation advocacy community continue to claim Section 106 review is far too bureaucratic and soulless. For them, Section 106 review does not advocate strongly enough for the protection of Historic Properties. Ironically, their opponents, those individuals and groups that marginalize the stewardship of our Nation's heritage in favor of narrowly construed private property rights, also challenge the validity of the process. They believe it is far too hostile to what they consider their sacrosanct entitlements to the unrestricted and most profitable use of their land and buildings.

Stoked by their antipathies against Section 106 review, zealots from both sides comb the collective of Section 106 cases for any instance where it appears that the process has failed. They seize upon those cases as vindication of their appeals to Congress to amend NHPA dramatically either to endorse their platform of required protection of Historic Properties at all cost, or to abolish the process altogether as being too 'big government'.

Therefore, any protracted, confrontational Section 106 case review will have an unfortunate secondary consequence of lending a seeming justification to the arguments of those persons and organizations in this country arrayed on either side of Heritage Stewardship who, for their own self-aggrandizing reasons, have continued to call the review process into question.

If for no other reason than this, those of us who esteem Section 106 review must continue to seek ways to reduce the volume and intensity of conflict within the process for it is our best long-term method so far devised for identifying Historic Properties and resolving Federal-project-related adverse effects against them.

SECTION 106 AND GAME THEORY

THE ULTIMATE RESOLUTION OF CONFLICT WITHIN THE 36 CFR 800 RULES: DRASTIC MEASURES

"We started off trying to set up a small anarchist community, but people wouldn't obey the rules."
- Alan Bennett

The 36 CFR 800 Regulation strongly encourages cooperation among all participants at every Step in the process. However, from the start, the ACHP Framers who drafted that Regulation were realistic enough to anticipate the possibility of conflict. They did their best to codify appropriate ways and means of resolving it within the scope of its rulebook.

The Regulation authorizes an Agency Official and an SHPO to consult with each other closely to take appropriate and coordinated steps whenever conflict does arise. These two primacy participants may:

1) agree to re-order the range of endgame payoffs in a manner that will appeal to all participants more readily, so long as they continue to identify, evaluate, and take into account Historic Properties

2) take all appropriate steps necessary to remind participants – if and when the need arises -- that Section 106 review is a process that melds the nation's historic preservation mission into the project-centered mission of the Federal Undertaking under review and that both missions have equal value

3) formally encourage reluctant participants to invest sufficient time and effort in becoming acquainted with the

goals and objectives of the other participants, their object being to break down stereotypes that impede cooperation

4) single out any participant who employs irrational or dishonorable strategies and hold that participant strictly accountable

Game Theory modeling makes it unmistakably clear that those players who hope to justify the standing they assume as participants in the Section 106 review process as well as the legitimacy of their actions during the run of the game must come to the table firmly committed to playing by the rules laid down at 36 CFR 800. They must be fully prepared with a rational set of pre-determined, well-defined, and rank-ordered goals derived by the employment of sound Utility Theory theorems. They must then heed the lessons taught by Prospect Theory, being both willing and able to modify those goals and/or their relative order of importance depending upon the observable actions of other participants as play progresses. They must be unstintingly willing to use the 'Tit for Tat' strategies of 'Symmetry and Parity' in their dealings with other players. They must be constantly ready to meet cooperation with immediate cooperation and non-cooperation with immediate non-cooperation.

The fact that the Agency Official and the SHPO are already primed by the language contained within the 36 CFR 800 Regulation to take these essential steps greatly improves the odds in favor of completing successful reviews marked by a true spirit of cooperation among the participants. Not taking them results in those cheerless negative payoffs that are the certain outcomes of competition, conflict, and non-compliant failure to agree.

CODA

"Just play. Have fun. Enjoy the game."
- *Michael Jordan*

I wrote this book because I believe the lessons learned from my investigations into the discipline of Game Theory can provide valuable guidance for those who wish to forestall conflict in Section 106 review. Game Theorists agree, for there to be 'honest games' there must be:

- **valuable payoffs, reasonably expected, and promptly attained**

I have already spent a fair amount of time discussing in detail the payoffs that players in Section 106 review can reasonably expect. Here is a summary. For the Agency Official, the payoff she desires most is prompt consensus with her determinations and findings from the other participants. For the SHPO, the highest payoff is the evaluation and protection of Historic Properties. For the THPO, the same payoff applies on Tribal land. For the Tribal representative, the same payoff applies off Tribal land. Other participants have their own easily-attainable payoffs that should naturally accrue to them during a normal Section 106 review case.

Because the Framers of 36 CFR 800 were well aware that time is money when dealing with Federal Undertakings, the Section 106 review process they created ensures that the vast majority (85%) of individual case reviews can be completed promptly within a finite number of short rounds (usually just two). Given the required suspense dates for SHPO responses to agency and applicant review requests, a typical Section 106 review should last no longer than one month from start to finish.

Furthermore, should SHPOs wish to foster an environment of cooperation with those whose Undertakings they review, they can do so quite easily by responding to review requests much more promptly than in the 30 days allocated to them.

- **a set of rational players who seek reasonable goals and use rational strategies to attain them**

Each participant in an individual Section 106 review case should welcome to the gaming table all others lodged within that pre-determined set of rational players, anticipating a well-defined and finite set of positive outcomes quickly arrived at. The process offers all participants a wide selection of rational and cooperative strategies to attain their goals and the flexibility to alter those strategies and goals as the game progresses.

- **free and continuing communication among all players**

Flexible and continuing communication is essential to successful completion of Section 106 review. Participants may bluff from time to time, but even a bluff is a form of communication. Participants who do not communicate with the others jeopardize any chance of attaining their goals.

- **low risk for all players as they themselves define risk**

Section 106 review does not require any participant to risk more value than he or she actually possesses in order to 'bid'. Put another way, the 'house limit' remains reasonable for all players. Cultural Resources *will* be identified, one way or another. Historic Properties *will* be evaluated, one way or another. Project-related effects *will* be assessed one way or another, and, if need be, adverse effects *will* be resolved, one way or another. The Federal Undertaking *will* proceed in one form or another.

- **commitment among all players to play by the rules**

In practical terms, this means each rational, intelligent participant in a Section 106 review case commits to exercise due diligence when bringing information, advice, and stated goals to the table.

Gaming the System

Even the best ruleset is subject to the irrational practice of 'gaming the system'. 'Gaming the system' means using the rules and procedures meant to protect a system in order, instead, to manipulate the system for a desired outcome. Irrational players in Section 106 review will use this strategy to forestall consensus among the other players in hopes of attaining their own desired outcome.

EXAMPLE: The 36 CFR 800 Regulation requires the Agency Official to ensure that the Section 106 process is initiated *early* in the Federal Undertaking's planning, so that a broad range of alternatives may be considered during the planning process for the Undertaking. Nearly all Agency Officials and applicants for Federal assistance abide by this rule because it is a reasonable requirement that is not particularly burdensome to them. However, this requirement opens a portal through which irrational players can move to challenge an Agency Official's timing. Agency Officials who initiate Section 106 review sufficiently early to satisfy long-standing best practices as certified by the SHPO may still be obliged to waste time and effort responding to the challenge of system gamers, as the definition of 'early' *is* subjective. However, **if** irrational players persist, **then** rational players will band together, re-assess the Agency Official's timing, and, almost always, come to stand with the Agency Official.

EXAMPLE: **If** more than one Federal agency is involved in an Undertaking, **then** some or all the agencies may agree among themselves to designate a 'lead Federal Agency' to represent them during the Section 105 process. Permitting agencies whose permit requirements overlap each other often designate one among themselves to be 'lead Federal Agency'. Irrational players game the system at times by arguing that the *wrong* Federal agency was designated lead. Their motivation to do so derives from their belief that they can delay continuation of consultation in this manner while the challenged Federal agencies ponder whether it is really necessary to waste time and effort re-considering their original assignment of lead.

The fact is that rational participants in Section 106 review hardly ever trouble themselves about which Federal Agency is lead in a Section

106 case. This being the case, they tend to band together to override this challenge, affirm the original selection, and get on with the case.

EXAMPLE: The Agency Official is obliged to use due diligence to plan her consultations in a manner appropriate to the scale of her Undertaking and the scope of Federal involvement. She is also obliged to coordinate that consultation with the requirements of other Federal statutes, as applicable. Rational Agency Officials who use discretion can normally be expected to meet these 36 CFR 800 obligations. Nevertheless, they still may find themselves challenged occasionally by irrational players claiming that, since an interpretation of the term "appropriate" is subjective, they have reason to believe that due diligence was not exercised.

Experienced, rational Section 106 review players familiar with best practices in this area have long since agreed upon an appropriate determination of scope and scale for most Federal programs that have the potential to affect Historic Properties. **If** an Agency Official meets that determination standard, **then** rational players will override this challenge as well.

Unfortunately, because of the wording of portions of 36 CFR 800, irrational players who search hard enough will find their share of opportunities to game the system. However, rational players with standing always seem to know what is at stake in Section 106 review. Therefore, they do their best to prevent gaming the system because they are aware that by doing so they risk losing that common positive endgame payoff which is the most valuable to them.

BTW. The Section 106 review system has its own well-earned reputation for gaming back when need be.

An 'Honest' Game

The Section 106 review process as codified at 36 CFR 800 is an archetypical example of an 'honest game' whose rules promote fairness and cooperation. These rules require participants to:
- consult freely throughout each case review
- prepare and review honest, thorough, and complete reports
- share the factual information derived from these reports openly
- seek consensus on accurate determinations of National Register eligibility, findings of project effect, and resolutions of adverse effect
- form alliances to further common goals, and
- fashion binding end-game commitments that memorialize the consensus they have reached

Nearly every one of the 70,000+ Section 106 review games in which I participated fielded an assemblage of rational participants who sought reasonable goals and used rational and cooperative strategies to attain them. They consulted among themselves freely and flexibly and they played strictly by the rules. In sum, they coordinated and cooperated splendidly with each other and with the process.

The positive payoffs for the participants in approximately 85% of these games resulted from consensus that no Historic Properties were affected by the Federal Undertaking being reviewed. The positive payoffs in an additional 13% came through consensus that the Undertaking would have no adverse effect upon identified Historic Properties. The positive payoffs in all but a fraction of the final two percent came through consensus concerning the best way adverse effect would be resolved.

Yet, despite the weight of Game Theory's overwhelming statistical evidence that coordination and cooperation among participants in games such as Section 106 review spawn timely, consistent, and successful outcomes, certain restive Section 106 review cases have still become mired in dispute and conflict, notwithstanding the clear guidance offered by the 36 CFR 800 Regulation.

For these few, there is still no choice other than resolution. To ensure procedural compliance with Federal law, they *must* be resolved satisfactorily, somehow. Under requirements codified at the 36 CFR 800 Regulation, the ultimate responsibility for resolving these restive cases has been assigned directly to the Agency Official and the SHPO who must consult together to end the game in a state of compliance.

THE TAKEAWAY

"We're all just playing our own game. I don't see it as a rivalry. We're just trying to play our best."
Michelle Wie

To sum up, this book has covered a great deal of ground concerning the art/science of Game Theory and its application with respect to the Section 106 review process, and especially with respect to conflict resolution within that process. Game Theory defines a 'game' as...

1) a series of interactions among rational, intelligent players who are
2) striving to make the best of a set of allowable moves, referred to as 'strategies' because these players are
3) motivated by a desire to attain certain goals referred to as 'payoffs' or 'utility functions', and

4) their goals and strategies for attaining these 'payoffs' are interdependent with the goals and strategies of the other players

Game Theory offers players a number of practical strategies:
1) create a common set of payoffs among all players
2) promote the free interchange of information
3) play strictly by the rules at all times
4) employ the strategies embodied in 'Symmetry and Parity' and 'Tit for Tat'
5) hold fast to the notion that cooperation rather than confrontation will ultimately ensure successful long-term compliance

The disciples of Game Theory continue to generate a set of mathematical models that buttress the hope that, **if** we can nurture a true spirit of cooperation within ourselves, **then** we can promote that same spirit among others. All this rhetoric about "true spirit of cooperation" may sound a bit wispy to those among us who see their 'winning' only in terms of someone else's 'losing'. Such ones tend to introduce conflict and confrontation into the mix at the very moment that cooperation seems to be gaining the upper hand. However it may appear, those of us committed to cooperation know *they* did not start that fight. *We* did.

There is a grand phrase that was delivered recently by my preacher, Steve Odom, that sums it up nicely. "We picked a fight with chaos." *We* decided to use whatever strategies that came to hand to bring order to this chaos in which we find ourselves at times. Game Theory seems to offer up some shrewd strategies for conflict resolution and prevention. That being the case, *we* will use them, and there is a better than even chance that *we* will win!

SECTION 106 AND GAME THEORY

My confidence in Game Theory modeling is firmly grounded in Cartesian analysis. Using this tool, Game Theorists have devoted the last five decades to the mathematical modeling that has derived winning strategies in some 29 "low stakes" games so far. They are analyzing various assortments of analogous "high stakes" games and winnowing out the ranges of choices that determine the types of payoffs that may come to rational participants. These analyses continue to be used with success worldwide by diplomats, generals, politicians, physical scientists, social scientists, religious leaders, and others whose business it is to advance light over darkness.

The salient point I am making here is, Game Theory provides useful and practical material for Agency Officials, applicants for Federal assistance, and SHPO Review and Compliance staffers that can enhances their mutual efforts to:

1) discern the difference between 'good' and 'bad' goals toward which to strive
2) rank 'good' goals in proportional order of utility
3) develop a flexible strategic approach to game play based upon coordination and interdependence with other players
4) modify the rank order of goals as the game moves forward
5) use flexible and honorable strategies, and,
6) reject dishonorable strategies

if you would rather agree with Seth Hoffman -- the famed American television producer and writer -- that rules are "just helpful guidelines for stupid people who can't make up their own minds," **then** Game Theory will teach you very little about overcoming the chaos that hovers over the Section 106 review process. However, my own years of relevant experience reaffirm the fact that, in the long run, the rules governing Section 106 review guarantee a game that rational participants can play cooperatively with confidence and can use Game Theory to win.

Participants in Section 106 review have the advantage of a rational and procedurally sound rule book plus the benefit of each other's consultation and help. Today and tomorrow, the profound lessons of Game Theory can teach these participants much as they attempt to minimize the harmful distraction of competition and conflict.

POSTSCRIPT

"Tell me and I forget. Teach me and I remember. Involve me and I learn."
- *Benjamin Franklin*

"You don't have to be a mathematician to have a feel for numbers,"
-*John Nash*

As should be obvious by now, this book merely skims the very surface of the surface of the discipline of Game Theory. Every author from whom I have borrowed has many additional weighty and useful observations to share about the interactions of rational individuals and groups and the best strategies for conflict resolution and prevention. Among those observations are some that may be even more helpful to you than those that appear here. These more nuanced observations carry far beyond the scope of this particular writing, and some of them are very likely far beyond the mental capabilities of this particular author. As I wrote earlier, we purveyors of the Section 106 review product are

SECTION 106 AND GAME THEORY

not usually of a mathematical turn of mind. Nevertheless, we can certainly learn something useful and practical from those who are.

This being the case, I heartily recommend that you do as I have done. Seek out these remarkable Game Theorists and their handy interpreters, consume as much of their work as you can, and absorb as many of their 'big ideas' as your non-mathematical minds will hold. You will profit from the effort, and so will your clients.

APPENDIX 'A'

A Case Study: A Section 106 Review Game Played According To The Rules Codified At 36 CFR 800.3-.6

"In the game of cricket, a hero is a person who respects the game and does not corrupt the game. The one who doesn't or corrupts the game, they are the villain."
- *Virat Kohli*

"Use soft words and hard arguments."
- *English Proverb*

Now it is time to put Game Theory and its principles to the test through the medium of a fictional case study that will showcase most of the features of Section 106 review that have the potential to provoke conflict. This case concerns the Federal Highway Administration (FHwA) and an FHwA-funded project proposed by the mythical State of TNT Department of Transportation (TNTDOT) in the county of Olive and the city of Olive City.

Case Study Overview

Here, we have a Federal Highway Administration (Federal Aid Highway Program funded), TNT Department of Transportation proposed, new-construction project ($17,000,000.00) for a 4.9-mile section of the proposed Olive Grove Connector in the City of Olive City, Olive County, TNT. TNTDOT proposes a new, divided, six-lane Interstate level highway with median and limited access connecting two of Olive City's major arterial surface streets (SR-409 and SR-549), at the latter's interchange with I-57.

Step One: Initiate The Section 106 Process:

Questions:

• What is the Federal agency's mission as demonstrated by the project under review?

One of the FHwA's key missions is to provide safe, efficient, and cost effective highways within the United States through the medium of Federal Aid Highway grant funds awarded to various state Departments of Transportation.

• Is this project an "Undertaking" subject to Section 106 review as defined in the 36 CFR 800 Regulation?

Almost five decades ago, the FHwA determined to initiate the Section 106 review process as codified at 36 CFR 800.3 (Step One) programmatically with respect to its Federal Aid Highway Program, because it had concluded that this program itself is an Undertaking as defined in the Regulation (800.3(a) and 800.9(a)). The FHwA did not make this determination to initiate Section 106 review of its various highway grants purely on its own or without benefit of wide-ranging consultation.

The 36 CFR 800 Regulation obliged the FHwA to determine whether or not its projects, programs, and activities are Undertakings subject to Section 106 review based upon the outcome of consultation with other stakeholders. It did so through consultation with various State Historic Preservation Officers, the National Conference of State Historic

Preservation Officers, the Advisory Council on Historic Preservation, a host of applicant state Departments of Transportation, representatives of Indian tribes, and many others.

The FHwA has consulted for many years concerning Section 106 review, and continues to do so. It has assured everyone concerned with *this* consultation that it will continue to remind its state DOT applicant of its responsibilities under Section 106. It will continue to emphasize those responsibilities having to do with: consulting with the appropriate State Historic Preservation Officer (SHPO), inviting additional Consulting Parties to participate, and formally notifying the public, thereby providing it an opportunity to express its concerns through public meetings.

The FHwA has agreed to notify each State Historic Preservation Officer of its designated "Agency Official" for each Undertaking. Here, the designated Agency Official for initial Section 106 review is the TNT Department of Transportation (TNTDOT) project administrator.

At the start of this Section 106 review game, the goal of the TNT Department of Transportation as designated Agency Official is to obtain prompt, low-risk, and consistent consensus from the other players. The TNTDOT candidly states this goal within its initial requests for Section 106 review by the TNTSHPO. For TNTDOT's payoff to be truly positive, consensus from the TNTSHPO and other participants must involve the least expenditure of its time, effort, and money.

The TNTDOT's strategy for attaining that goal at this point is cooperative; to play strictly by the rules, to accomplish this goal promptly, and to emphasize the relevant facts contained within its review request documentation that support its determinations of National Register of Historic Places eligibility and its findings of project-related effects. Beyond Section 106 review, the ultimate goal of the TNTDOT is the prompt receipt of its FHwA awarded funding for its proposed project with the lease expenditure of its own money, time, and effort. Its strategy at this point remains cooperative; to provide the TNTSHPO and the other players with adequate, accurate, and consistent documentation concerning this Undertaking in hopes of generating a speedy and positive response from the other participants.

- What is the size and nature of the Undertaking as defined in the Regulation?

Proposed is a 4.9-mile new-construction section of the Olive Grove Connector that the TNTDOT has designed as a divided six-lane Interstate level highway with median, providing limited access, and connecting two of Olive City's major arterial surface streets (SR-409 with the SR-549 interchange to I-57).

- How will the Federal agency notify the appropriate State Historic Preservation Officer?

Upon determining that the Federal Aid Highway program for a specific fiscal year is an Undertaking as defined in the National Historic Preservation Act (NHPA), the FHwA, through its applicant, the TNTDOT, will notify the TNT State Historic Preservation Officer that it has initiated the Section 106 process (800.16(f), 800.3(c), 800.3(f), 800.3(f)(1) and 800.3(f)(2)).

The 36 CFR 800 Regulation permits the FHwA to take this initial notification step in one of two ways. It may, on its own by a direct consultation request, begin Section 106 consultation. It may also initiate the process indirectly through a review request initiated by a duly certified applicant for its highway funds. It has chosen the second option to begin Section 106 consultation through an initial review request from its applicant state DOT.

In return, the TNT State Historic Preservation Officer is obliged to acknowledge in writing either a Federal Highway Administration direct consultation request or a duly certified state Department of Transportation's review request within thirty days.

The FHwA also has the option to coordinate Section 106 review with other required environmental reviews (800.3(b)) such as National Environmental Policy Act (NEPA) review. The 36 CFR 800 Regulation presents this option to Federal agencies in the interests of streamlining Federal review processes and reducing duplication of effort.

The 36 CFR 800 Regulation clearly encourages Federal agencies to meld Section 106 review into other relevant environmental review requirements such as those imposed by NEPA. For example, Federal agencies may use NEPA documents such as Environmental Assessments (EA) and Environmental Impact Statements (EIS) to document their Undertakings for purposes of Section 106 review. Federal Agencies may also use NEPA endgame documents such as Findings of No Significant Impact and Records of Decision to satisfy Section 106 review. This is the case so long as such documents were the product of due consultation as defined in the 36 CFR 800 Regulation. To ensure that NEPA documents satisfy the requirements of Section 106 review, Federal agencies such as the FHwA have done the following:

- develop a common set of project documents that satisfies the stated documentation needs of all pertinent review authorities including the State Historic Preservation Officer
- develop and implement a policy document that clearly asserts that certain projects and programs categorically excluded from National Environmental Policy Act review or other statutory environmental review are not necessarily exempt from Section 106 review

Federal agencies such as the FHwA must always keep in mind that NEPA documents such as EAs and EISs are usually promulgated relatively late in a project's planning and environmental review cycle. Therefore, any agency wishing to meld Section 106 review and NEPA review risks a finding by the State Historic Preservation Officer that further consultation is irrelevant should it surmise that the agency submittal of the EA or EIS is the SHPOs first and only awareness of the Undertaking. It is best for agencies such as the TNTDOT to initiate Section 106 review long before beginning the preparation of NEPA documents.

Federal agencies such as the FHwA that elect to delegate initial Section 106 review responsibility to their applicant state DOTs should consult programmatically with the appropriate SHPO before doing so. The FHwA should provide the SHPO with mutually agreed upon certification notices that it has delegated initial Section 106 review contact. Typically, Federal agencies accomplish this by:

- A blanket written notification that lists its designated applicants and/or application packagers or consultants
- An individual certification letter attached to each applicant, packager, or consultant review request
- Some other mutually-agreed-upon means

Absent Federal agency certification, the SHPO may wish to consider applicant requests as technical assistance requests rather than true Section 106 requests for consultation and to provide whatever information the SHPO has at hand to satisfy the request. However, no one should consider any such technical assistance responses as binding Section 106 consultation under the 36 CFR 800 Regulation.

The initial goal of the TNTSHPO in this particular Section 106 review is to assist, advise, and cooperate with the TNTDOT as it defines the Undertaking, assembles a roster of Consulting Parties, formulates its plan for involving the public, and renders its National Register determinations and effect findings. The TNTSHPO's strategy at this point is cooperative; to be prompt and forthcoming in responding to the TNTDOT's requests for assistance and advice.

The ultimate goal of the TNTSHPO is to ensure that Historic Properties located within the state of TNT are identified, evaluated, and protected to the extent possible under the provisions of Section 106. The TNTSHPO's cooperative strategy is to provide the TNTDOT with any useful information held by the SHPO to facilitate the identification and protection of known Historic Properties and to be on guard against possible errors, omissions, or inconsistencies in the Agency Official's supporting documents.

- How will the public be involved?

The FHwA or its applicant, the TNTDOT, will involve the public in the Section 106 process (800.3(e), 800.2(d)(1) and 800.11(c)). As is the case with Consulting Parties, The FHwA or the TNTDOT will consult with the TNTSHPO respecting a method for involving the public. This method should demonstrate a good faith attempt to take the public's views on preservation issues into account.

The 36 CFR 800 Regulation requires the FHwA or its applicant to provide basic information to the public relative to:

- The existence of Historic Properties within the Undertaking's possible Area of Potential Effects (but not necessarily their exact location)
- The general nature of the potential for project effect upon these Historic Properties

The FHwA may utilize its existing procedures for informing the public based upon Federal law, Regulation, or internal policy document. Such procedures should be commensurate with proper identification of Historic Properties within the project's possible Area of Potential Effects and evaluation of project effect.

The primary goal of the public at this point is to inform itself concerning the proposed Undertaking and to make known any concerns relative to it or to any identified Historic Properties affected by it. This is especially true with respect to the TNTDOT. The public's strategy at this point is cooperative; to express those concerns in written communications of one sort or another and to attend public meetings where concerns may be discussed and transcribed and consensus sought.

- How will the other likely Consulting Parties be assembled?

The FHwA, through the offices of the TNTDOT, and the affected SHPO will consult together to identify other appropriate Consulting Parties (800.16(f), 800.3(c), 800.3(f), 800.3(f)(1) and 800.3(f)(2)). The FHwA or the TNTDOT will invite all agreed-upon Consulting Parties to participate in the consultation process.

The FHwA or the TNTDOT shall take the views of all Consulting Parties into account. Consultation with all Consulting Parties runs through the entire Section 106 review process.

The primary goal of any identified Tribal Historic Preservation Officer (THPO) at this point is to identify and protect Historic Properties of cultural or religious significance to the tribe located on tribal lands affected by this Undertaking, if, and only if, the Undertaking is proposed on tribal lands. The THPO's strategy at this point is cooperative; to notify the Agency Official if there are known significant Historic Properties that may be affected by the proposed Undertaking without necessarily divulging the location of those Historic Properties and to advocate for their protection and to be on guard against errors, omissions, or inconsistencies in the Agency Official's supporting documents.

The primary goal of affected representatives of local government at this point is to represent the best land use interests of each affected local government relative to the Undertaking and associated Historic Properties. Their primary strategy is cooperative; sharing with the other participants any information they may have regarding local Cultural Resources designations, land use policies, and so forth and supporting or opposing the Agency Official's determinations and findings based upon an assessment of their compatibility with local land use interests.

The primary goal of affected property owners at this point is to obtain the fullest and best use of their property. Their strategy is either to support or oppose the Undertaking based upon its ability to meet that goal.

The primary goal of those Consulting Parties who have a legal or economic relation to the Undertaking at this point is to protect their legal or economic interest. Like affected property owners, these players' strategies involve supporting or opposing the Undertaking based upon those interests.

At this point, the primary strategy of those Consulting Parties who are concerned with the Undertaking's effects on Historic Properties is cooperative; to identify and protect any Historic Properties that may be affected by the Undertaking. Their secondary strategy involves supporting or opposing the Undertaking based upon its effect on Historic Properties.

The primary goal of affected tribal representatives at this point is the identification and protection of Historic Properties of cultural or religious significance to the tribe off tribal lands. Their strategy is cooperative; to notify the Agency Official of any known significant Historic Properties that may be affected by the proposed Undertaking without necessarily divulging the location of those Historic Properties.

As game play moves into the second, third, or fourth round, these initial goals and strategies may or may not shift, depending upon the cautions described earlier in the section of the book devoted to Prospect Theory. Each player will make the appropriate combination of moves that form that pattern most likely to attain for him or her the most positive payoffs.

Step Two: Identify Historic Properties:

SECTION 106 AND GAME THEORY

Questions:

- What is the Federal agency's scope of effort for this project as defined in the Regulation?

The FHwA, through the offices of its designated Agency Official (TNTDOT), will consult with the TNTSHPO and will agree upon an appropriate project Area of Potential Effects (APE) and identify any Cultural Resources located within its boundary.

First, in consultation with the TNTSHPO, the TNTDOT will "determine and document the Area of Potential Effects, as defined in 36 CFR 800.16(d)". The FHwA has the final word on the boundary of the APE, but it rarely differs from any consensus reached by its DOTs and the SHPO.

Second, in consultation with the TNTSHPO, the TNTDOT will "review existing information on Historic Properties within the Area of Potential Effects, including any data concerning possible Historic Properties not yet identified." The TNTDOT will also consult with the TNT state archaeological laboratory and the state site file repository. If the TNTSHPO staff archaeologist and/or archaeological site file curator determine that there are no known or suspected archaeological resources within the project APE, he/she/they will so document that determination to the TNTDOT. If known or suspected archaeological sites are located within the APE, he/she/they will so document that determination to the TNTDOT. In this case, the state archaeological laboratory and the state site file repository may well add that an archaeological Cultural Resources survey should be conducted to identify and evaluate archaeological resources within the APE for their National Register eligibility.

Third, the TNTDOT should "seek information, as appropriate, from Consulting Parties, and other individuals and organizations likely to have knowledge of, or concerns with, Historic Properties in the area, and identify issues relating to the Undertaking's potential effects on Historic Properties". This means that the TNTDOT should seek guidance and information on the proposed right-of-way acquisition site from the Olive County Executive and the Olive County Historian, among others.

Fourth, the TNTDOT should "gather information from any Indian tribe identified pursuant to 36 CFR 800.3(f) to assist in identifying properties, including those located off tribal lands, which may be of religious and cultural significance to them and may be eligible for the National Register. This requirement recognizes that an Indian tribe may be reluctant to divulge specific information regarding the location, nature, and activities associated with such sites." The FHwA should warn its applicants concerning confidentiality issues pursuant to 36 CFR 800.11(c).

If consultation with a tribe concludes that there are no known sites of cultural or religious interest to the tribe located within the project APE, the TNTDOT should notify other Consulting Parties of that fact.

Fifth, the TNTDOT should "identify Historic Properties based on the information gathered in consultation with the State Historic Preservation Office and any Indian tribe that might attach religious and cultural significance to properties within the Area of Potential Effects". The TNTDOT should then "take the steps necessary to identify Historic Properties within the Area of Potential Effects."

This means requesting such information from any Indian tribe that may have a religious or cultural interest in the land being set aside for the highway project right-of-way. If the tribe has previously assured the TNTDOT in writing that it knows of no such sites, then the TNTDOT should communicate that fact to the SHPO.

Finally, the TNTDOT should "make a reasonable and good faith effort to carry out appropriate identification efforts, which may include background research, consultation, oral history interviews, sample field investigation, and field survey." The TNTDOT should, "take into account past planning, research and studies, the magnitude and nature of the Undertaking and the degree of Federal involvement, the nature and extent of potential effects on Historic Properties, and the likely nature and location of Historic Properties within the Area of Potential Effects." The *secretary of the interior's standards and guidelines for identification* provide guidance on this subject. The TNTDOT should also consider other applicable professional, State, tribal, and local laws, standards, and guidelines. The TNTDOT must take into account any confidentiality concerns raised by Indian tribes during the identification process."

In practical terms, this means that the TNTDOT's Cultural Resources staff should conduct or have conducted a Cultural Resources survey of the project APE that takes into account the cultural and religious interests of tribes.

- What is this project's APE as defined in the Regulation?

The appropriate project APE for this type of highway project usually consists of a direct APE that includes all areas where right-of-way is to be acquired, buildings or structures are to be erected or demolished, and ground is to be disturbed plus an indirect APE that comprises a linear APE measuring in width ½ mile each side of the proposed project centerline.

- What is the likelihood of identifying Historic Properties within the APE?

If there are known Cultural Resources located within the direct APE (archaeological and architectural resources) and/or the indirect APE (architectural resources), then there is a strong likelihood of the existence of Historic Properties. The Cultural Resources survey report will identify and evaluate these Cultural Resources.

Everyone associated with this evaluation process should note "the passage of time, changing perceptions of significance, or incomplete prior evaluations may require the [Consulting Parties] to reevaluate properties previously determined eligible or ineligible."

- How will Cultural Resources be identified?

The TNTDOT will identify any Cultural Resources located within the project APE through consultation with the TNTSHPO and other Consulting Parties including affected tribes, and through the preparation of appropriate Cultural Resources surveys by architectural historians and archaeologists who meet the secretary of the interior's professional qualifications.

- How will Historic Properties be evaluated?

The TNTDOT will evaluate the National Register eligibility of any identified Cultural Resources located within the project's APE in consultation with the TNTSHPO, and the other Consulting Parties, and the author of any required Cultural Resources survey reports.

Once a Cultural Resources survey report has been prepared and reviewed, "in consultation with the State Historic Preservation Officer and any Indian tribe that attaches religious and cultural significance to identified properties and guided by the secretary's standards and guidelines for evaluation, the TNTDOT shall apply the National Register criteria found at 36 CFR 63 to Cultural Resources identified within the Area of Potential Effects that have not been previously evaluated for National Register eligibility."

If this consultation determines any of the National Register criteria are met [respecting any Cultural Resource identified in the survey] and the SHPO agrees, that Cultural Resource shall be considered eligible for the National Register for Section 106 purposes. If the consultation determines the criteria are not met and the SHPO agrees, the Cultural Resource shall be considered not National Register eligible.

If there is disagreement respecting the eligibility of an identified Cultural Resource, the Federal Highway Administration shall obtain a determination of eligibility from the secretary [through the Office of the Keeper of the National Register of Historic Places] pursuant to 36 CFR 63. If an Indian tribe that attaches religious and cultural significance to a property off tribal lands does not agree, it may ask the Advisory Council on Historic Preservation to request the Federal Highway Administration to obtain a formal determination of eligibility from the Keeper.

As stated earlier, during this game-play round of Step Two consultation, certain participants might disagree concerning the size and scope of the APE based upon their own differing initial goals. For example, after comparing his two possible initial goals of...

1) concurring with the TNTDOT's delineation of the project's APE in order to facilitate cordial relations with a sister state agency and,

2) challenging the TNTDOT's delineation of the project's APE because of his more-universal goal of augmenting his knowledge of and information about Cultural Resources in the vicinity of the proposed Undertaking...

...the TNTSHPO opted for a larger APE than the one submitted by the TNTDOT.

Contrariwise, after comparing her two goals of...

1) providing the TNTSHPO with Cultural Resources information covering an expanded APE and,

2) saving a portion of the money, time, and effort allocated to the preparation of an expanded Cultural Resources Survey Report...

...the TNTDOT project administrator opted for a more tightly-drawn APE than usual.

At this point, the TNTDOT and the TNTSHPO each 'bid' their preferred 'come to the table' goal, and these goals obviously did not coincide. Then, each player had a choice; 1) to hold tenaciously to that initial goal, thereby creating conflict that would endanger the prospect of successful completion of the review, or 2) to consult further and modify their original goal in response to the activities of the other player.

Prospect Theory suggests a viable solution as it urges game participants constantly to re-assess their own goals and those of the other players as well.

Interdependent and candid consultation between the TNTDOT and the TNTSHPO uncovered the underlying reasons each player selected his or her 'come to the table' goal. Out of this consultation emerged a cooperative strategy that saved the TNTDOT money, time, and effort by limiting archaeological investigations to the actual footprint of the proposed highway and supplementing relevant TNTDOT architectural site file data with more recent SHPO-generated data while still affording the TNTSHPO a certain amount of additional information about Cultural Resources located within the project's APE by expanding the indirect APE to ¾ mile from the centerline.

Both players had rejected the dishonorable strategies of fallacious argument in favor of emphasizing the relevant facts in support of each 'player's' own statements. Furthermore, both players had been candid with each other when consulting about why they chose their initial goals, freely exchanging honest and pertinent information. Both had been willing to acknowledge that each had put forward a reasonable argument in favor of their initial goal. Both had been willing to modify their original goal based upon interdependent interactions with each other as play moved along through Step Two.

In this instance, each player had decided how their modified goal could coincide with, and not clash with, the goal of the other. Both the TNTDOT and the TNTSHPO had played strictly by the rules laid down at 36 CFR 800, each knowing that this particular game of Section 106 review would end cooperatively and successfully at whatever round was appropriate if and only if all its players had accepted the existence of a common set of payoffs that would reward each of them in some fashion, while punishing none severely.

Through interdependent consultation, both the TNTDOT and the TNTSHPO did reach consensus on the size and scope of this project's APE. This consensus produced a common payoff that achieved a positive and significant portion of each player's 'come to the table' goal while inflicting only a small negative payoff on each.

However, at this point in Step Two consultation, participants in a Section 106 review game might also sometimes disagree over the 'facts' contained within the Agency Official's supplementary documentation package.

The TNTDOT's Cultural Resources survey report identified three architectural Cultural Resources and two historic archaeological Cultural Resources. From this baseline, the TNTDOT determined that one of the three architectural resources is National Register eligible and one of the archaeological resources is National Register eligible.

For his part, through the use of in-house TNT Cultural Resources survey files of the area, the TNTSHPO determined that two of the three architectural Cultural Resources and both of the historic archaeological Cultural Resources are National Register eligible.

At this point, the TNTSHPO might well 'raise' the stakes in the game by requesting the TNTDOT prepare additional documents, survey reports, etc. and he might even propose to make a site visit to verify the 'facts on the ground'. If the TNTSHPO remains dis-satisfied with the results of the TNTDOT's supplemented determination of National Register eligibility, then he might even 'raise' yet again through a petition to the ACHP to invoke a Formal Determination of Eligibility from the Keeper of the National Register of Historic Places.

From this point, play cannot end successfully, or even continue to the next round of the game until the issue of National Register eligibility has been resolved one way or the other. Still, if both players continue to consult in good faith and play strictly by the rules codified at 36 CFR 800, the Section 106 review game can continue to proceed compliantly.

In this instance, the Keeper ruled that two of the architectural Cultural Resources *are* National Register eligible and one of the historic archaeological Cultural Resources is eligible. Both the TNTDOT and the TNTSHPO agreed to abide by this finding. However, that did not end the matter because the current highway project calls for the removal, by one means or another, of certain designated archaeological and architectural Cultural Resources within the APE.

Any demolition of a National Register *eligible* Historic Property requires an automatic adverse effect finding. (At this point, and for the sake of argument, I am going to stipulate that the TNTSHPO and the TNTDOT have already concurred that there are no prudent or feasible alternatives to the current project location.) However, the project's right-of-way corridor is wide enough to allow the TNTDOT some leeway in placing the footprint of the highway with the result that it has some choice as to which Historic Properties it will remove.

Now, because of the relative locations of the evaluated Historic Properties along the direct and indirect APE, the TNTDOT has a choice of A) demolishing the two architectural Historic Properties and avoiding the historic archaeological Historic Property or B) data recovering the historic archaeological Historic Property and avoiding the two architectural Historic Properties.

Alternative 'A' assumes a cost of $5,000 for each demolition, plus a combined Historic American Building Survey (HABS) -level photo-documentation cost of $2,000 by way of mitigation of the adverse effect / total $12,000.

Alternative 'B' assumes a mitigation cost of $7,000 for the data recovery of the historic archaeological site / total $7,000.

The TNTDOT assigned Alternative 'A' -12 value points because of the proportionate extra money it must expend during Step Four associated with the requirement to resolve the adverse effect through mitigation of the two Historic Properties. The TNTDOT assigned Alternative 'B' only -7 value point because it will cost proportionately less money in data recovery mitigation during Step Four adverse effect resolution.

At this point, with all other project-related conditions being equal, and mindful of the budgeting associated with the relative costs, the TNTDOT opts for Alternative 'B' as the preferred alternative.

Therefore, based solely upon considerations of budget, the TNTSHPO determined to bid Alternative 'B' as its preferred mitigation of the adverse effect.

However, when reviewing the various levels of significance of the affected Historic Properties, the TNTSHPO determined that the historic archaeological Historic Property was an intact, regionally-significant, 19th. Century Tent Meeting Site (+8 points) that should be avoided by the highway project if at all possible while the two architectural Historic Properties were marginally-eligible remnants of a locally-significant early 20th. Century farmstead (+2 points). Therefore, the TNTSHPO opted for Alternative 'A' as its preferred alternative.

At this point, when faced with the TNTSHPO's counter-bid, the TNTDOT re-assessed its original assignment of value points in the selection of a preferred alternative. In the end, with the support of the FHwA, the TNTDOT decided to change its preferred alternative to Alternative 'A" and absorb the extra expenses associated with highway re-design as a cost of doing business. The TNTSHPO's revelation about the relative 'value' of the Historic Properties located within its project's APE was supremely influential in altering the TNTDOT's determination because of that agency's commitment to 'enlarging the shadow of the future' with the TNTSHPO.

Step Three: Assess Project Effects:

Questions:

• What is the nature and extent of potential effects to Historic Properties as defined in the Criteria of Adverse Effect codified at 36 CFR 800.5?

Under the Federal Aid Highway program, the FHwA allocates funds to selected states to finance a broad range of highway widening, new construction, and bridge repair and replacement projects among other things. All such programs have the potential to affect Historic Properties eligible for listing in the National Register of Historic Places. This particular Undertaking is no exception.

• What is the result of applying the Criteria of Adverse Effect to the project under review?

The 36 CFR 800.5 Regulation states that an adverse effect is found when an Undertaking may alter, directly or indirectly, any of the characteristics of a historic property that qualify the property for inclusion in the National Register in a manner that would diminish the integrity of the property's location, design, setting, materials, workmanship, feeling, or association. An Agency Official must give consideration to all qualifying characteristics of a historic property, including those that may have been identified subsequent to the original evaluation of the property's eligibility for the National Register. Adverse effects may include reasonably foreseeable effects caused by the

Undertaking that may occur later in time, be farther removed in distance or be cumulative.

Adverse effects on historic properties include, but are not limited to:

(i) Physical destruction of or damage to all or part of the property;

(ii) Alteration of a property, including restoration, rehabilitation, repair, maintenance, stabilization, hazardous material remediation, and provision of handicapped access, that is not consistent with the Secretary's standards for the treatment of historic properties (36 CFR 68) and applicable guidelines;

(iii) Removal of the property from its historic location;

(iv) Change of the character of the property's use or of physical features within the property's setting that contribute to its historic significance;

(v) Introduction of visual, atmospheric or audible elements that diminish the integrity of the property's significant historic features;

(vi) Neglect of a property which causes its deterioration, except where such neglect and deterioration are recognized qualities of a property of religious and cultural significance to an Indian tribe or Native Hawaiian organization; and

(vii) Transfer, lease, or sale of property out of Federal ownership or control without adequate and legally enforceable restrictions or conditions to ensure long-term preservation of the property's historic significance.

The TNTDOT, the FHwA, and the TNTSHPO reviewed the TNTDOT's proposed functional drawings for the proposed new highway right-of-way in light of the identified Historic Properties located within the direct and indirect APE. The result of that consultation was a mutually agreed upon finding that the project as currently proposed would physically destroy the two architectural Historic Properties thus resulting in a direct adverse effect and provide increased, unprotected access to an intact, regionally-significant, 19th. Century Tent Meeting Site thus resulting in an indirect adverse effect.

- Which Criteria of Adverse Effect apply to this project?
    1.) Physical destruction of or damage to all or part of the property, and
    2.) Change of the character of the property's use or of physical features within the property's setting that contribute to its historic significance
- Is there a true public interest imperative in this specific Undertaking?

At some point in their planning process, all Federal projects, programs, and activities must 'justify their existence' somehow or other. This particular Undertaking is no exception. In planning this new highway construction, the TNTDOT roadway planning, design, and engineering staff had to respond to a very specific purpose and need for this project. After studying the traffic needs of the area, they designed a new, divided, six-lane Interstate level highway with median and limited access connecting two of Olive City' major arterial surface streets (SR-409 and SR-103), at the latter's interchange with I-57).

The purpose and need for such a new highway segment is quite apparent from the TNTDOT's design proposal. Exponential population growth in Olive City over the past two decades has overwhelmed the city's major crosstown arterial surface streets, which also happen to be state highways. These surface arterials can no longer move traffic safely and swiftly from one side of Olive City to the other. Furthermore, local traffic congestion along these arterials interferes with the smooth flow of intrastate traffic. There is a definite need to syphon off a large portion of this crosstown traffic through the construction of a limited access connector that will allow both local and intrastate traffic to flow smoothly. The design of the connector envisions controlled access at its termini and only a few necessary traffic signals, limited access cross lanes, and turn lanes, as they tend to retard traffic flow along the route. Furthermore, since the new highway is slated to intersect one of these surface arterials right at its interchange with an Interstate Highway, the design of the new highway section must be at an Interstate-comparable level to absorb the Interstate highway traffic out flow onto the surface streets and accelerate the surface street traffic influx onto I-57 safely.

In summary, there is a clear public interest imperative for this project.

At this point in the case study, a reader may well ask, "Why did you wait till now to ask this very important question about public interest imperative?" The answer is quite simple. Had this Section 106 case review concluded with a determination of "no Historic Properties affected" or even "Conditional No Adverse Effect", the public interest imperative associated with the heritage stewardship mission of the Section 106 review process would not have been challenged because no Historic Properties would have been threatened. In such cases, the State Historic Preservation Officer would be obliged to take the Agency Official's assurances of the necessity of the project under review at face value.

However, once consultation among the Agency Official, SHPO, and other Consulting Parties results in an adverse effect finding, then all parties to the review are obliged to weigh the relative public interest imperatives of the project against those of heritage stewardship. In such cases, the public interest imperative of heritage stewardship reflected in the language of the National Historic Preservation Act compels Agency Officials to use due diligence in seeking and evaluating those project alternatives that might avoid or minimize that adverse effect. These alternatives must take into account the original project's purpose and need while at the same time remaining fiscally prudent and feasible.

Step Four: Resolve Adverse Effect:

Questions:

- Can the adverse effect be avoided?

This specific case happens to be one of the very few in which the adverse effect to Historic Properties cannot prudently or feasibly be avoided. The termini of the new highway are fixed by the existing locations of the two arterials it is designed to connect. Therefore, the proposed line of highway between its beginning and end points cannot be removed away from those Historic Properties it will adversely affect and still retain its purpose and need.

In a perfect world where money is no object, one might propose building an overpass along the entire route that would be designed to avoid the Historic Properties. However, given the current fiscal resources of the FHwA, such an alternative is certainly not prudent, and may not even be feasible.

Candid and interdependent consultation between the TNTDOT and the TNTSHPO has validated the conclusion the agency used due diligence in its investigation of alternatives that would have avoided project-related adverse effect and the adverse effect cannot be avoided.

- Can the adverse effect be minimized?

Consultation between the TNTDOT and the TNTSHPO consequent to the adverse-effect-resolution requirements codified at 36 CFR 800 has minimized the adverse effect of this project significantly. Originally, the TNTDOT had declared that its preferred alternative was Alternative 'B' that called for the data recovery of the archaeological Historic Property and the avoidance of having to demolish the two architectural Historic Properties. However, further consultation caused the TNTDOT to reject Alternative 'B' in favor of Alternative 'A' once the TNTSHPO informed it of the high level of significance of the archaeological Historic Property and the relatively-low level of significance of the two architectural Historic Properties. The resulting minimization of the project's adverse effect required the TNTDOT to budget more funds than it had originally intended to mitigate the adverse effect.

Such changes made by Federal agencies and applicants for Federal assistance do much to justify the Section 106 review process and its heritage stewardship mission.

- Can the adverse effect be mitigated?

Continuing consultation between the TNTDOT and the TNTSHPO has resulted in a standard and sound mitigation of the demolition of two architectural Historic Properties through HABS-level documentation. One must remember, however, that the demolition of the two marginally-eligible buildings instead of the data recovery of a highly-significant archaeological site is also a mitigation of a certain kind. Together, these two elements comprise a mitigation package wholly satisfactory to the TNTSHPO and also lend credence to his faith that future consultations with the TNTDOT will be fruitful.

A RECAP

The case study just reviewed jibes exactly with our definition of a 'Category Three' game. It involves a series of interactions between rational players (the TNTDOT and the TNTSHPO) where the winner is the last player to move. Both players began the game with specific goals, then freely and interdependently cooperated with each other according to the rules of the game by employing a set of allowable and honorable strategies that dramatically reduced their risk of failure. During game play, they modified their original goals to comport with the changing nature of the game. This allowing them to attain a common set of valuable and positive 'payoffs' at the end of game play.

Both players refused to allow themselves to be stalemated in a Nash Equilibrium. Instead, they used the strategies of 'Symmetry and Parity', 'Reciprocity', and 'Tit for Tat' to keep the game alive. They immediately met each 'bid' of cooperation with a counter bid of cooperation and each 'bid' of non-cooperation with one, and only one, counter bid of non-cooperation in expectation that, in the long run, cooperation would prevail, which it did. Both the TNTDOT and the TNTSHPO strove to enlarge the shadow of the future by proving to each other that they were trustworthy over the long run and sympathetic to each other's fiscal, time management, and policy constraints. Both followed a policy of cooperation -- Game Theory's most important lesson – by establishing focal points that will render Section 106 consultation even less risky in future cases.

Those agencies and individuals involved in Section 106 reviews can reduce the risk of non-compliance whenever they use the lessons of Game Theory to influence game play in ways that nourish cooperation among its players. In this way, they will find common goals that preserve both the Federal agency mission and the heritage stewardship mission.

APPENXIX 'B':
Game Theory And Section 106 Quick Reference

Introduction

This book considers how State Historic Preservation Office Environmental Review and Compliance (R&C) staffers, and Federal Agency Officials, and applicants for Federal assistance can best use the analysis of the Section 106 review process made possible by modern Game Theory to assist them in preventing those conflicts that occasionally erupt out of their cases. Furthermore, I believe all those additional Consulting Parties named in the Section 106 review rulebook (36 CFR 800) will also benefit from the information contained in this book.

The Federal Regulation / 36 CFR 800 / Section 106 ruleset provides for:

1) A Federal Agency Official
2) Various other participants (ACHP, Consulting Parties, and the Public)
3) Four successive rounds of play
4) Support documentation definitions
5) Allowable determinations and findings
6) Allowable ranges of strategies
7) Allowable sets of outcomes

Game Theory Definition

"That branch of mathematics concerned with the analysis of strategies for dealing with competitive situations where the outcome of a participant's choice of action depends critically upon the actions of other participants".

'Analogous Predictive Analysis' Definition

Analogous Predictive Analysis extracts information from the data set of known 'low stakes' games and uses it to predict trends and behavior patterns in analogous 'high stakes' games whose function is similar and comparable while admittedly having different origins.

Rational Player Definition

One who chooses her goals and strategies based upon an awareness of her best possible expected payoff, given her knowledge of the game-related situation at the time those choices were made and also the choices of the other players.

Brinkmanship Definition

Brinkmanship requires a player (Superpower "A") to employ a strategy of ever-escalating threats against his opponent. These threats are clearly perceived by the other player (Superpower "B") as hostile. This second player responds in his turn and escalates his own threats against his opponent.

Modern Game Theory Definition

Modern Game Theory, inspired by Charles Leonard Bouton, Oskar Morgenstern, John von Neumann, Thomas C. Schelling, and others, focuses on real life examples and analyzes 'low stakes' games that are analogous and therefore relevant to the 'high stakes' games encountered in daily life.

'If-Then Statement' Definition

The 'if' part of the statement, or the hypothesis, places a tentative condition, qualifier, or caveat on the 'then' part of the statement; the conclusion. If the condition is false, then the conclusion will also be false. If the condition were true, then the conclusion will also be true.

Dominated and Dominant Strategies Definition

1) 'Dominated' strategies (never win, no matter what any other player does)
2) 'Dominant' strategies (always win, no matter what any other player does)

Game Theory Words and Section 106 Review

1) Board: The game board upon which the game is played. In Section 106 review, the board is the figurative consultation table around which all participants sit.
2) Capture: A method for removing another player's game pieces from the game board that is compliant with the rules of that game. The

SECTION 106 AND GAME THEORY

example board game used in this book where capture is the object is NIM. It's pieces represent various stages in a specific Section 106 review.

3) Turn/Move: A player's opportunity within the rules of the game either to move a game piece or to make a 'bidding' decision. In Section 106 review, the Agency Official always makes the first move, and the State Historic Preservation Officer/Tribal Historic Preservation Officer (SHPO/THPO) and other participants move in turn in response.

4) Pass: A forfeiture of a turn by a player. If the SHPO does not respond to a formal submission by the Agency Official of her determinations and findings within the 30 days allowed by the rules of the game, the Agency Official may assume a pass and continue to the next round of the game.

5) Call: A player's formal settlement to end a round of game play through mutual agreement with the other player. The SHPO may 'call' the Agency Official's formal submission of determinations of findings by reaching consensus and so notifying the Agency Official.

6) Pie Rule: A rule, which if agreed upon by both players, eliminates any advantage of moving first. After the first players' opening move, the second player has the option of swapping sides to take up where the first player left off. There is no Pie Rule in Section 106 review.

7) Rule: A condition, convention, or stipulation by which a game is played. The rules of Section 106 review are ordained by the NHPA and are separately codified at 36 CFR 800.

8) Ruleset: The comprehensive set of rules that define game play and govern a game. The ruleset for the game of Section 106 review is 36 CFR 800.

9) Best Play: The strategy (or strategies) which produces the most favorable outcome for a player, taking other players' strategies as a given. In Section 106 review best play eventuates in a common payoff beneficial to all participants.

SECTION 106 AND GAME THEORY

Goal Definition

A goal is a player's 'utility' or positive payoff (the highest possible value or the lowest possible risk)

Strategy Definition

1) A 'good' strategy is one most preferable to attaining a positive payoff.
2) A 'bad' strategy is one least preferable to attaining a positive payoff

Utility Theory Attributes

1) Goals and strategies are comparable (better/worse).
2) Goals and strategies are transitive (better/worse, better/worse).
3) Indifference to payoffs translates into indifference to the rules of the game.
4) A player will gamble when tempted by good odds of achieving a desired goal.
5) A player will stay in a game with multiple rounds only so long as he feels that the ultimate payoff will attain his desired goal and that the corresponding reward is truly valuable.

Jake Nielson's Checklist for Ordering Goals and Strategies

1) Define the Players
2) List the possible goals and strategies available to each player
3) Create a Scenarios Matrix
4) List how much each player values each goal or strategy in a Payoff Matrix

Prospect Theory Attributes

1) A player assigns value to perceived possible gains over time differently from the way in which she assigns value to perceived possible losses based largely upon intuition.

2) That player's intuitions grow out of a sense of 'availability' or the ease with which a particular idea can be brought readily to mind, and 'representativeness' as seen when people allow pre-judged stereotyping categories or pigeonholing to sway their decision making.

Rational/Honorable Game Strategies in Section 106 review

1) Emphasize relevant facts in support of the player's own determinations and findings
2) Emphasize errors or omissions in another player's determinations and findings
3) Emphasize completeness and accuracy in the player's own supporting documents
4) Emphasize errors, omissions, or inconsistencies in another player's supporting documentation, and
5) Bluff for strategic reasons

Irrational/Dishonorable Game Strategies in Section 106 review

1) Resort to rhetorical tricks as an appeal to human emotion against fact and reason
2) Use fallacious arguments in an attempt to deflect attention from the real issues being discussed
3) Delay merely for the sake of delay
4) Fake evidence to support an irrational player's position

Honest Players According to Mike Gene

1) Do not overstate the power of their own argument
2) Are willing publicly to acknowledge that reasonable alternative viewpoints exist
3) Are willing publicly to acknowledge and question their own assumptions and biases
4) Are willing publicly to acknowledge where their argument is weak
5) Are willing publicly to acknowledge when they are wrong
6) Demonstrate consistency in their statements
7) Address the argument instead of attacking the person making the argument
8) Do not misrepresent an argument, either their own or another 'player's
9) Demonstrate a commitment to critical thinking
10) Are willing publicly to acknowledge when a criticism of their argument is valid

Game Theory Maxims

Each Rational and intelligent player should be able to:

1) Compare, rank, select, and communicate their pre-determined goals before play begins

2) Adopt honorable strategies for achieving their goals

3) Adapt their original goals and strategies based upon interdependent interactions with other players as play moves along from one round to the next

4) Cooperate with other players to attain binding agreements that reflect positive payoffs

5) Make decisions in agreement with his own wishes

6) Communicate openly with the other players.

7) Determine whether his goals agree with or clash with those of other players.

8) Decide at any given point in game play whether to cooperate or compete with other players.

9) Play strictly by the cooperative rules of the game

10) Seek to secure certain rewarding payoffs through a 'binding agreement' with the other players.

11) Use the game to manipulate circumstances while in full knowledge that circumstances are manipulating him at the same time.

12) Find a game to be increasingly resistant to Game Theory's predictive modeling as it 1) becomes more nuanced; 2) absorbs increasing amounts of time and effort; 3) increases risk.

Inducements in Section 106 Review

1) The primary inducement is obviously supplied by the statutory and regulatory requirement that Agency Officials. SHPOs, THPOs, Tribal

Representatives, and a host of other participants must seek each other out and continue to consult until resolution has been reached.

2) An important inducement to remaining in a game of sequence such as Section 106 review must be the promise of an eventual positive payoff.

3) The extent to which the rules of a game allow and even encourage players to communicate with each other during the course of play is directly proportional to their willingness to stay in the game.

4) The opportunity and the encouragement to modify strategies and goals is yet another inducement.

Restrictions in Section 106 Review

1) The general restrictions imposed by the 36 CFR 800 ruleset
2) The mandated order of play
3) A plausible threat made by one of the players
4) The limitations imposed by endgame agreements

Common Knowledge Definition

Common knowledge is knowledge that is known by everyone or nearly everyone, usually with reference to the specific community in which the term is used.

Focal Points Definition

Game Theorists refer to those places, times, and circumstances considered more or less 'common currency' by us all as 'Focal Points' or 'Schelling Points'.

SECTION 106 AND GAME THEORY

Influences That Pre-Determine the Course of the Game

1) The relative values or 'utilities' of the final payoffs
2) The 'attraction of distraction'
3) The rational (or irrational) manner of game play
4) The level of freedom afforded by the game
5) The cooperative or competitive personalities of the players
6) The ancillary risks

Home Truths That Pre-Determine the Course of the Game

1) If and only if all its players have accepted the existence of a common set of payoffs that will reward each of them in some fashion, while punishing none severely, then a game will end cooperatively and successfully at whatever round is appropriate.

2) If they expect to win in the long term, then all participants in the review game must play fairly and strictly according to the rules, both formal and informal.

3) If the Agency Official attempts to foster an atmosphere of free interchange of information among participants, then she will have taken a major step toward cooperative, mutually-beneficial completion of the process.

4) A Consulting Party who acts cooperatively, even if the proposed Undertaking threatens a Historic Property, will reassure the Agency Official that he is willing to consult further to seek common solutions that will protect the resource as much as possible while fulfilling the Undertaking's mission.

5) If Consulting Parties demonstrate their awareness of the ancillary risks associated with carrying out the Undertaking under Section

106 review, then they will accumulate much good will and a cooperative attitude from the Agency Official responsible for implementing that Undertaking.

Graphical Tools

The Decision-Payoff Matrix

A Challenge to Game Theory: Professor Stanley K. Ridgley

1) Multi-player games impose too much 'background noise' that confuses players' ability to comprehend the actions of other players.
2) Not all game players are rational.

Acknowledged Limits of Game Theory

1) The more players, the more complex the strategy becomes.
2) The more nuanced the game, the more difficult it is to identify its most positive goals.

Trusting Game Theory's Usefulness in Section 106 Review

1) The proof of analogous predictive analysis lies within Game Theory's record of accomplishment
2) Players must be assured of the right utility and the right strategy for attaining it. Utility Theory offers such assurances.

SECTION 106 AND GAME THEORY

3) Enlightened by the tenets of Prospect Theory, rational participants will come to understand the need to re-define their own highest utilities and accompanying strategies during each game.

4) Once a participant feels his re-defined strategies will attain his highest value payoffs, he should seek to identify those goals shared with other players through interdependent consultation.

Is Section 106 Review Really a Game?

Section 106 review easily meets the definition of a game because it is:

1) a series of ordered (as defined at 36 CFR 800.3 through .6) interactions among rational players:

    a) a Federal Agency Official (or an applicant for Federal funds, licenses, permits, or approvals)
    b) a State Historic Preservation Officer (SHPO)
    c) a Tribal Historic Preservation Officer (THPO)
    d) Tribal Representatives or Native Hawaiian Organization Representatives
    e) Representatives of local government
    f) Affected property owners, and
    g) Individuals or groups with standing because of economic interest or historic preservation interest in the Federal Undertaking under review.

2) These players are striving to make the best of a set of allowable moves (strategies) codified at 36 CFR 800.

3) They do so because they are motivated by the desire to attain certain goals that they bring to the consultation table.

4) These goals are interdependent with those of the other players.

The Common Goal

The Common Goal is the successful completion of the process.

Categories by Object of the Game According to Arthur T. Benjamin

1) Category 1: Winning is amassing the most stuff.
2) Category 2: Winning is completing some sort of structure or ordered pattern.
3) Category 3: Winning is being the last player to move.

Section 106 Review Is a Game of Sequence

1) Opening Gambit (establishing qualifications to play, taking possession of one's assigned portion of the game board, receiving one's initial set of tokens or cards, placing forced antes, if required, into the 'pot', making opening moves to 'test the water')
2) Midgame (discovery of opponent strategies, analysis and re-ordering of one's own strategies, maneuver, and counter-maneuver)
3) Resolution or Endgame (final showdown) that awards payoffs

Section 106 Review Catalogued by Type

1) Meant to be cooperative rather than competitive
2) Not a 'zero-sum' game
3) A 'sequential' game
4) A game of 'imperfect information'

5) A game of random strategies
6) Not a 'combinational game'
7) Completed within a finite number of moves and counter-moves
8) Composed of a finite number of players

The Rounds and The Moves Within Rounds List in Detail

1) Initiate the Section 106 Process
- Establish Undertaking
- Identify Appropriate SHPO/THPO
- Plan to Involve the Public
- Identify Other Consulting Parties
2) Identify Historic Properties
- Determine Scope of Efforts
- Identify Historic Properties
- Evaluate Historic Significance
3) Assess Adverse Effect
- Apply Criteria of Adverse Effect
4) Resolve Adverse Effect
- Continue Consultation

The Section 106 Review Game: The Players List in Detail

1) The Federal Agency Official tasked with the responsibility of implementing a Federal Undertaking subject to Section 106 review

2) The Advisory Council on Historic Preservation (ACHP) tasked with the responsibility of monitoring whether the rules of the Section 106 review game are followed

3) The State Historic Preservation Officer (SHPO) tasked with the responsibility of assisting, advising, and cooperating with the Agency Official as she identifies, evaluates, and takes into account the Cultural Resources and Historic Properties located within the Undertaking's APE

4) The Tribal Historic Preservation Officer (THPO) tasked with the responsibility of identifying, evaluating, and protecting the significant cultural and religious resources located on his tribal lands

5) The authorized representatives of Indian tribes and Native Hawaiian Organizations tasked with the responsibility of identifying, evaluating, and protecting significant cultural and religious resources located off tribal lands

6) The authorized representatives of local governments tasked with the responsibility of representing the 'best land use interests' of their jurisdictions

7) The applicants for Federal funds, licenses, permits, and approvals of one sort or another, tasked with the responsibility of obtaining that assistance promptly and with the least possible risk

8) The affected public and private property owners, tasked with the responsibility of obtaining the best and fullest use of their properties

9) The other parties with a specific economic interest in a Federal Undertaking that affords them standing

10) The other parties with a specific historic preservation interest in a Federal Undertaking that affords them standing

11) The Public

Nash Equilibrium Definition

A Nash Equilibrium is achieved when competing players have all chosen strategies by which they try to attain their goals (payoffs), where no individual player believes he or she has anything to gain by changing his or her own strategy so long as the other players do not change their own strategies.

'Symmetry and Parity' Definition

1) Symmetry is defined as "similarity or exact correspondence between different things". Another definition emphasizes the state of being symmetrical; that is, corresponding in size, shape, and relative position to parts on opposite sides of a dividing line or median plane or about a center or axis. Symmetry is a state of being in balance and correspondence.
2) Parity is defined as "the state or condition of becoming equal". Another definition emphasizes the state of becoming equally odd or even as compared with another.
3) The key difference between the two concepts lies in the fact that parity is a state of becoming equal while symmetry is a state of being equal.

Specific Lessons Learned from Arthur T. Benjamin

1) Lesson# 1: Use the 1/3 Bluff Formula
2) Lesson# 2: Thwart Irrational Players And Contested Games
3) Lesson# 3: Break It Down
4) Lesson# 4: Work Backwards
5) Lesson# 5: Reject The 'Greedy' Strategy

A Vindication of Cooperation In Game Theory: Robert Axelrod

SECTION 106 AND GAME THEORY

1) Axelrod arranged a computer competition, pitting some of the world's foremost Game Theorists against each other. The winning entry was submitted by Anatol Rapoport (May 22, 1911–January 20, 2007), then at the University of Toronto. Rapoport's winning strategy may be summarized quite neatly in that timeworn kids' way for dealing with disputes on the playground; 'Tit for Tat'. Axelrod held a second tournament to see if anyone could find a better strategy. 'Tit for Tat' won again!

2) 'Tit for Tat' is an effective strategy that begins any game with an opening 'bid' of either cooperation or confrontation. Thereafter, the player using this strategy does exactly what his opposite number did in the previous round.

3) In Section 106 review, Agency Official cooperation is immediately met with SHPO/THPO cooperation, just as it is immediately met during a Fourth Grade recess period. Agency Official non-cooperation is immediately met with SHPO/THPO non-cooperation. Admittedly, the SHPO/THPO makes his non-cooperative response in the sincere hope that it will encourage the rational Agency Official to return to a cooperative posture so that the process may continue smoothly and promptly toward compliant completion.

'Tit for Tat' and 'Symmetry and Parity'

A bid in Symmetry is met with a Parity bid that keeps the board in Symmetry while an Asymmetry bid is also met with a Parity bid that also returns the board to Symmetry.

The Evolution of Cooperation: Robert Axelrod

Robert Axelrod maintains that a spirit of cooperation among the rational participants in a game will evolve once it is made known to them that cooperation is their proven best long-term mutual strategy.

The Cooperative Personal Environment

1) Don't be envious
2) Don't be the first player to 'defect'
3) Reciprocate both cooperation and defection
4) Don't be too clever

The Cooperative Game Environment

1) Enlarge the shadow of the future
2) Change the payoff
3) Teach people to care about each other
4) Teach reciprocity
5) Improve recognition abilities

The Most Important Lesson

Cooperation among rational players is mathematically more likely than competition to generate sustainable goals and attain rewarding payoffs for all.

Over The Long Haul

1) 'Tit for Tat' depends upon the promise of an eventual state of mutual cooperation in order to attain a final win/win for each of a game's participants.

2) Game Theorists see all rational players as acting this way because of the power of mutual self-interest. They also admit that irrational players do not necessarily act this way. In those instances, they state unequivocally that the tenets of Game theory do not apply.

3) Game Theory emphasizes the notion that those rational participants in a Section 106 review case who seek common ground with other participants through cooperative consultation that forms alliances are more likely over the long haul to attain their goals and receive the payoffs they desire. The more cooperation among the participants exists, the greater chance of mutual reward.

Chaos Theory

1) 'Sensitivity to Initial Conditions' proposes that an arbitrarily small initial change in the current path followed by either a projectile or a process within a system may lead to a significantly different future outcome as against the previous path.
2) The passage of time causes a decrease in predictability

The Takeaway

Game Theory offers players a number of practical strategies:
1) Create a common set of payoffs among all players
2) Promote the free interchange of information
3) Play strictly by the rules at all times
4) Employ the strategies embodied in 'Symmetry and Parity' and 'Tit for Tat'

5) Hold fast to the notion that cooperation rather than confrontation will ultimately ensure successful long-term compliance

www.ingramcontent.com/pod-product-compliance
Lightning Source LLC
Chambersburg PA
CBHW080616190526
45169CB00009B/3206